# Hannah Moore

Best wishes to Joyce

Isabel B. Weigold

November 17, 2007

# Hannah Moore

## A Biography of a Nineteenth Century Missionary and Teacher

Her story is one of courage, dedication,
and religious fervor as revealed in her letters
from the Dwight Mission in Oklahoma
and the Kaw Mendi Mission in West Africa dating
from 1833 to 1868

Isabel B. Weigold

iUniverse, Inc.
New York  Lincoln  Shanghai

**Hannah Moore**
**A Biography of a Nineteenth Century Missionary and Teacher**

Copyright © 2007 by Isabel Weigold

iUniverse books may be ordered through booksellers or by contacting:

iUniverse
2021 Pine Lake Road, Suite 100
Lincoln, NE 68512
www.iuniverse.com
1-800-Authors (1-800-288-4677)

Because of the dynamic nature of the Internet, any Web addresses or links contained in this book may have changed since publication and may no longer be valid.

The views expressed in this work are solely those of the author and do not necessarily reflect the views of the publisher, and the publisher hereby disclaims any responsibility for them.

ISBN: 978-0-595-43135-9 (pbk)
ISBN: 978-0-595-87480-4 (ebk)

Printed in the United States of America

Dedicated to the memory of

my husband

Harold Wallace Weigold

# CONTENTS

# ACKNOWLEDGMENTS

Many people have encouraged and assisted me in my efforts to research and write Hannah Moore's story. I am indebted, first of all, to Dr. Carol Nutile Burke, who volunteered, on numerous occasions, to drive me to Yale University and to the Connecticut State Library. She helped review microfilm letters and documents and research relevant books, and she was a constant source of encouragement when the research seemed to lag.

To Laura J. Quackenbush, curator of the Leelanau Historical Museum in Leland, Michigan, who tracked down the name and address of a visitor to her museum some years before, who was also interested in Hannah Moore. As a result, I was able to contact Rev. William Knott, a Seventh-day Adventist minister, who provided a great deal of information regarding Hannah's decision to become a Seventh-day Adventist and her experiences in Battle Creek. His magazine article on Hannah's life in 1998 and his doctoral dissertation entitled "Foot Soldier of the Empire: Hannah More and the Politics of Service," provided new insights which he was willing to share.

I am indebted to Dr. Ruth Moynihan for her encouragement and expert advice, both of which resulted in substantial improvements in the depth and organization of this book.

Thanks are due to Jeannine M. Upson, Union's town historian, who provided pictures of Union's churches, schools, and houses as well as information about the town's early history.

And finally, I very much appreciate the cooperation and assistance of the staffs at the Yale Divinity School Library, the Yale University Library, the Houghton Library at Harvard University, the office of the County Historian, Oswego County, New York, the University of Tulsa, the University of Oklahoma at Norman, the Old Sturbridge Village Library, Sturbridge, Massachusetts, and Roberta Passardi, librarian for the Willington Public Library.

# INTRODUCTION

In searching through a folder of letters in the Willington Historical Society's archives, I found a letter from Hannah Moore addressed to "Dear Sisters Eldridge" dated August 31, 1852. The return address was Kaw Mendi, West Africa, which meant nothing to me, but as I continued reading, I was interested to realize that Hannah was a missionary, and the only white woman, there. However, my curiosity was immediately aroused when I read the words "the return of the Amistad," because the movie *Amistad* had just been released and had been receiving a tremendous amount of attention, particularly in Connecticut where much of the filming took place.

Other than this letter, I could find nothing to connect Hannah to Willington. A search of the vital records at the State Library indicated that there were several Hannah Moores, but it was also possible she might not have been born in Connecticut at all.

I had no idea when I started that it would lead to more than five years of research, uncovering 150 letters written by Hannah or about her. I would learn that she was not only a missionary for six years in Africa, but actually began her missionary career in the wilds of Oklahoma, long before it became a state. She taught Cherokee and Choctaw Indian children to read and write, just a few years after their tribes' enforced and arduous journey, aptly referred to as the "Trail of Tears."

The movie *Amistad* concentrated on the capture and final release of Cinque, a Mendi native, and thirty-six Africans, but did not attempt to tell the story of what happened to these men and women after the trial. Three years elapsed before they were able to accumulate the funds necessary to buy passage back to West Africa. Several had died in Connecticut, and others decided not to return. Of the original thirty-six Mendi natives, several deserted once they arrived in Africa, leaving fourteen to go with William Raymond to establish the Kaw Mendi Mission.

Although Hannah was not the first of the female missionaries to serve at Kaw Mendi, she was one of a group that arrived soon after George Thompson, who replaced William Raymond in 1847. This, then, is Hannah's story as reflected in her letters and through the letters of others who knew her at the time. Perhaps more than that, it is a story of a missionary's life, first in Oklahoma and later in Africa, thousands of miles from home, in a land where tribal warfare was rife, and in a time when little thought was given to the life-threatening conditions with which she had to contend. This is a story of courage, dedication, and religious fervor in the face of adversity within and without the mission.

# Chapter One: "Tuesday's Child Is Full of Grace"

Born in Union, Connecticut, on Tuesday, November 22, 1808, Hannah Moore's destiny as a child "full of grace" would become apparent to her mother early on, as we will see. Named for her grandmother, Hannah (Crocker) Whiton, she was the sixth of ten children born to Samuel and Amy (Whiton) Moore in the old homestead on Stickney Hill Road. The farm, covering more than 150 acres, had been inherited by Samuel and had been in the family since 1739 when Samuel's grandfather, James, who emigrated from Ireland to Grafton, Massachusetts, purchased the property just five years after Union was established.

The last town east of the Connecticut River to be settled, Union is situated in the northeastern part of Tolland County, bounded on the north by Massachusetts, on the west by Stafford, on the east by Woodstock, and on the south by Ashford. Rocky, hilly, and heavily forested, with, for the most part, unproductive soil, there are no major streams, but there are the many brooks that unite with the Willimantic and Quinebaug rivers. Mashapaug Lake, (the Indian name for "great water") located a short distance from the Moore farm, is a beautiful expanse of water covering about eight hundred acres. Hammond, in his "History of Union, Connecticut" described Union as the highest town east of the Connecticut River and added, "the people of this town live a little nearer heaven than any of their neighbors."

When Hannah was a young girl, the town boasted thirteen sawmills, several shoe factories, axe handle factories, and a tannery. In a letter to her sister, Joanna, she referred to an incident that suggests she worked in either a woolen or a cotton mill that existed in the 1820s and '30s, and was probably located in nearby Stafford Springs.

If Hannah were to return to her hometown today, she would find the mills gone without a trace, but the town grove, with its white-steepled church would be relatively unchanged. The old homestead in which she was born either burned or was taken down and another house erected in 1837 on the same property. After her mother died, her father lived with his son Samuel Whiton Moore and his family until his death in 1861. Their farmhouse, depicted below, shows the building as it appeared in the 1990s.

**Samuel Whiton Moore house built circa 1837 on Stickney Hill Road**
Photo courtesy of the Union Historical Society

**The Thomas Moore farmhouse built circa 1785 on Moore Road**
Photo courtesy of the Union Historical Society

Thomas Moore, Hannah's great uncle, built the farmhouse pictured above which still stands, a silent witness to more than two hundred years of Union's history.

Hannah's family, all ardent followers of Congregationalism, faithfully attended the church on the town common every Sabbath. Although it is neither the same structure where Hannah and her sisters, Anna, Sophia, Lucinda, Joanna, and Lydia were baptized by Rev. David Avery in 1815, nor the one she joined in 1829, the present building, erected in 1833, would have been attended by Hannah when she came home to visit.

No letters or journals exist to indicate what Hannah's life was like in those early days. But it is well-known that life was not easy for a farmer and his family in the nineteenth century. This was especially true in Union where the ground had to be cleared of trees, glacial boulders, and rocks before crops could be planted. The stone walls built by Samuel Moore and the other farmers still stand today, snaking their way through the forests, lining the roadways, and marking property boundaries.

Managing a large farm required the help of the entire family. Samuel and Amy had six children, five girls and one boy, who was the youngest. Because there were no older brothers to help with the farm, Hannah and her sisters were expected to help with all aspects of farming. They worked in the kitchen, did the laundry, brought in wood for the fireplace, spun and wove material for their clothing and bedding, fed the chickens, collected eggs, fed and milked the cows, and helped with the haying in the summer.

Sunday was strictly observed as a day of rest. Other than feeding the animals and milking the cows, all other activities were suspended for the day. The family attended the Union Congregational Church, which was approximately five miles away, so they would be gone for a good part of the day. There were usually two church services—one in the morning, which lasted about two hours, followed by lunch and a shorter service.

Although there are no copies of Rev. David Avery's sermons in existence, it can be assumed that Hannah, who described herself as a "deeply religious child," would have been impressed by the idea that one could only be saved from the fires of hell by confessing one's sins, repenting, and praying for salvation. Some years later, in a letter to Rev. David Green, secretary of the American Board of Commissioners for Foreign Missions (ABCFM), Hannah wrote: "I had many seasons of reflection on the mutability of all things earthly and the vast importance of being ready for death."

In 1818, when Hannah was ten years old, a new religious movement was underway, called the Second Great Awakening. This was a time of religious revival and a renewed commitment to the religious tenets. Although none of Hannah's letters allude to being influenced by the rhetoric of this new movement, it is highly likely that the Moore family would have attended a series of meetings at the Union church conducted by Asahel Nettleton, the most famous evangelist in the state. His message was abundantly clear—confess your sins, yes, but go forth and preach the gospel so that others might be saved as well. This idea marked the beginning of the missionary movement and may have had a part in Hannah's decision to become a teacher/missionary.

**Union Congregational Church, at right, is the second building erected near the site where Hannah was baptized. The building on the left is the Town House built in 1847.**
Photo courtesy of the Union Historical Society

# Chapter Two: From Common School to Dudley Academy

When Hannah first began school is not known, but children usually started at the age of six. She attended the school in the Northwest District, which was one of six school districts in Union. Each school was located close to the center of the district so that children were within walking distance. Accompanied by her older sisters, Hannah walked about a mile to the one-room school over a rough, rock-strewn path.

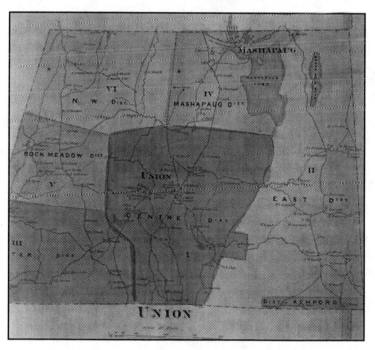

**Map showing School Districts in Union, Connecticut.**
**Hannah attended school in District VI.**
Map taken from the Atlas of Windham and Tolland Counties,
Connecticut published by Baker and Tilden 1869

The early schools, often painted red, were usually about twenty-two by thirty-two feet in size. The entry hall was furnished with shelves for the dinner pails and wooden pegs for hanging the children's wraps. A pail of water with one dipper was placed in the hallway. Children were seated on benches made from oak boards without backs, facing the teacher's desk, which was slightly elevated at the front of the room. Each family in the district was expected to take turns furnishing wood for the fireplace. Textbooks were scarce for the most part, so teachers gave oral lessons or used homemade textbooks.

No record exists of the teachers for the years when Hannah attended school, but it was common practice to hire a male teacher during the winter and a female during the summer months. The number of students in each of the district schools varied, but the average was about twenty-five students ranging in age from six to eighteen.

In addition to the core subjects such as arithmetic, penmanship, spelling, and reading, children were also taught personal habits of cleanliness, punctuality, obedience, and diligence. Children were expected to memorize information so that it could be recalled exactly the way it was read or heard. Assimilation of the information would come later. Those who learned by association or other means floundered in this environment unless the teacher was astute enough to recognize individual differences in learning styles.

Hannah had a prodigious memory judging from the testimony of Rev. Charles Hammond, also from Union, and the principal of Monson's Academy in Monson, Massachusetts, who cited her remarkable ability to repeat three or four hundred verses of scripture at one time. Elijah Eldridge, with whom Hannah boarded when she taught in Willington, also referred to Hannah's ability in a letter to the ABCFM. "I think she is better acquainted with the Bible than any woman I know of and poseses (sic) a good memory."[1]

Career opportunities for women in the nineteenth century were extremely limited, compared to the opportunities available today. Hannah and her sister Joanne had experienced working in a local mill, which Joanne referred to as noisy and dirty. It was also unhealthy, forcing many young women to quit due to lung congestion (brown lung) caused by the inhalation of cotton or wool dust.

Teaching was another possibility, but, in general, it was expected that young women would marry and raise a family. Hannah, however, had other ideas. She felt called to the missionary field, where she could do more than just teach; she could be instrumental in saving the souls of the heathens, as well.

---

1     Capt. Elijah Eldridge to Mr. David Green, October 9, 1840, ABCFM (Houghton)

As early as 1833, Hannah wrote to Rev. William S. Porter, director of the Nichols Academy in Dudley, Massachusetts, to ask for a recommendation to the ABCFM, knowing that its goal was to promote the spread of the gospel in heathen lands. Dominated by Congregationalists, the Board sent missionaries to the West as well as overseas to India, Ceylon, Hawaii, and China. But, apparently, it was reluctant to send single women to isolated western posts and suggested she could do much good as a New England school teacher instead of as a missionary. She replied, "I am not needed here. If the Board should not need my services, I have thought of applying to the American Home Missionary Society or the Sunday School Union."[2]

Hannah must have received information from the ABCFM indicating that she did not meet their educational requirements. She knew she could not depend on her parents for financial assistance, so she turned to teaching to earn her tuition. She obtained a teaching position at the Village Hill School in Willington, a short distance from Union, and boarded with one of the town's leading citizens, Captain Elijah Eldridge. Eldridge owned and operated a number of mills on Roaring Brook, one of which made wooden rakes that were renowned for their quality.

She saved enough money to enroll at Dudley Academy (also referred to by Hannah as the Nichols Academy) in nearby Dudley, Massachusetts, where she completed two terms while earning her keep with outside work from 1832 to 1833 and another three terms between June 1838 and March 1839. She studied mental philosophy, arithmetic, grammar, and composition, according to a letter she wrote to the American Board of Commissioners on September 28, 1839.

Hannah boarded with a local family during at least one of her terms at Dudley. In a letter to her sister Amy she wrote: "The hardest of the work seems to devolve on me." The family owned six cows, all of which were apparently milked each day by Hannah—they were "not Union cows," for "some of them have given a pail full of milk at a time," she wrote. She found that the physical labor was far more tiring than her schoolwork: "I thought when I first began I should have to give out," she wrote. "I have got so tired & had such a back ache." "I loved all my studies much," she recalled, "I never failed in writing my grammatical exercises or desired an excuse when Compositions were required." As she became adjusted to the demanding schedule of hard labor and the required schoolwork, she found her health improving and boasted to her sister that she was meeting the expectations of a religious female living away from her family. For she had "staid

---

2    Hannah Moore to Rev. Daniel Green, October 1, 1838, ABCFM (Houghton)

(sic) from meeting only two Sabbaths," and was an active member of the Dudley Congregational Church's Sabbath School.

Rev. William Porter, director of the Dudley Academy, in a letter of recommendation to the American Board in 1833 reported Hannah to be "a very respectable scholar." "She is prudent, judicious, retiring, of ardent though missionary piety, economical & industrious and highly respected by all."[3]

Five years later there was still no doubt in Hannah's mind that she was destined to become a missionary. "I have for more than a year felt a strong degree of faith or belief that I shall ere long enter the field of missionary labor," she wrote to the ABCFM on October 1, 1838. "I think, if I am not greatly deceived, I have a call from a higher power than any earthly tribunal to engage heart and hand in the work of the mission, to carry the glad news of salvation to the benighted heathen who are perishing for lack of knowledge."[4]

Hannah's decision to become a missionary may also have been reinforced by her association with other students at Monson Academy who were also planning to become missionaries. She was undoubtedly acquainted with young, zealous Samuel Marsh, who graduated in 1840 and sailed to South Africa to preach the gospel to the Zulus. Perhaps she was stirred even earlier by stories told by her great uncle, Samuel Whiton, who had served as a missionary in South Africa and later worked in Home Mission fields in the western part of the United States.

Letters of recommendation were required as part of the application process to become a missionary under the auspices of the ABCFM. Two of these letters reflect differing opinions about her teaching ability and particularly classroom discipline. Captain Eldridge wrote, "There was a very grate (sic) attachment to her of her pupils and their parents and she exerted a good influence over them." On the other hand Rev. Samuel Curtis, of the Willington Congregational Church, wrote to the ABCFM stating that "she punished the little children severely and repeatedly" after promising their parents she would be more mild.[5]

Hannah believed in the "spare the rod and spoil the child" method of discipline which was, undoubtedly, what she experienced as a child both at home and in the schoolroom. However, when she attended Dudley Academy, she would learn about a different approach as espoused by Rev. Charles Hammond, who

---

3    Rev. William S. Porter to Secretaries of the ABCFM, May 8, 1833, ABCFM (Houghton)

4    Hannah Moore to Rev. Daniel Green, October 1, 1838, ABCFM (Houghton)

5    Rev. Samuel Curtis to David Green October 12, 1840, ABCFM (Houghton)

fervently believed that physical punishment was unnecessary and that classroom discipline could be attained by isolation or verbal remonstrance.

Judging from her comments about discipline as early as 1839, Hannah was aware that physically punishing pupils worked for some and not for others. She wrote: "Everything depends on the wisdom, fairness, prudence and direction of the teacher," for with some pupils, "the rod and reproof seem needed to give wisdom."[6] While Hannah seemed to understand that there was more than one way to maintain order in the classroom, she would, more often than not, rely on physical punishment for which she was criticized in Willington and later in Oklahoma and Africa as well.

Having attained the additional education required and, perhaps, because of her continued and unabated correspondence, the ABCFM finally, in February of 1841, appointed Hannah to the Dwight Mission in the Oklahoma Territory.

---

6     Hannah Moore letter to Secretaries ABCFM dated February 25, 1841 (Houghton)

# Chapter Three: Indian Territory

After several months of delay, at the age of thirty-one, under the aegis of the ABCFM, Hannah made her way to the Indian Territory, which later became the state of Oklahoma.

Rev. David Green, secretary of the ABCFM, had difficulty finding suitable companions to accompany Hannah on the proposed fifteen-hundred-mile journey from New York City, through Philadelphia, Pittsburgh, and Cincinnati, and down the Ohio River to the Mississippi River, but Hannah was not deterred. She reminded the secretary, "When I am told I need some one to accompany and protect me, I tell them I know that I do, an unfailing Friend, 'who sticketh closer than a brother,' & with such a protector I need not fear."[7]

After several months' delay, she left from New York City and, much to the relief of her parents, she was accompanied by Mr. and Mrs. Jared Olmsted, a missionary couple traveling to the Choctaw Nation. After an uneventful trip, the Olmsteds left Hannah at Little Rock, Arkansas, where she continued alone up the Arkansas River through Fort Smith and Fort Coffee, arriving at the Sallisaw Landing in the Cherokee Nation in the dark of night.

Arrangements had been made for her to stay overnight with a family named Payne who lived at the landing. Because of their light-colored skin, Hannah was under the impression she was staying in a home owned by white people and asked her host in the morning if he could speak Cherokee. She was embarrassed to discover that it was his native tongue and realized that her preconceived ideas of Indians needed to be revised.

In a letter dated October 20, 1841, addressed to Rev. Green, secretary to the American Board, Hannah described her ten-mile journey by horseback to the Dwight Mission:

> I found this wilderness had indeed budded and blossomed with the roses, which were in full bloom when I came. I was delighted in passing through the first Prairie I ever saw—it was the season of the year

---

7    Hannah Moore to Rev. David Green, February 25, 1841, ABCFM (Houghton)

when all nature seemed blooming with beauty and emitting its richest odours. It very forcibly reminded me of the time when my moral night was turned to spiritual day.

Everything appeared so different, even the trees and plants & flowers wore an aspect and were very different from what I had seen in Connecticut. Still, I felt I could say "My father made them all," & under his guidance & protection I felt as safe as I should at home. I felt the cause I was about to engage in was worth the sacrifice. Though I had tasted keenly the parting pang, the farewell & adieus were past.

The Dwight Mission was named for Timothy Dwight, president of Yale College in New Haven, Connecticut, and a well-known minister and educator as well as a corporate member of the ABCFM. The first Mission was established in 1820 by two ordained ministers and two assistants: Rev. Cephas Washburn, Rev. Alfred Finney, Jacob Hitchcock, and James Orr. They came in response to a request from Chief Tahlonteskee of the Western Cherokee Nation, who had been impressed with the school and the work of the ABCFM.

Cephas Washburn was born in Randolph, Vermont, in 1795. He graduated from the University of Vermont in 1816, was licensed to preach in January 1818, and, ten months later, married Abigail Woodward, also of Randolph. He preached in small Vermont towns until October 1818 when he and his wife left New England for the state of Georgia. He served the Savannah Missionary Society as agent for one year and then decided, in 1816, to accept an opportunity to work among the Western Cherokees. Reverend Finney, a graduate of Dartmouth College, married Rev. Washburn's sister, Susanna. Unfortunately, Rev. Finney died within a month after arriving at their new location in 1829.

Jacob Hitchcock was of pioneer Massachusetts stock and had learned a number of trades. Deeply religious, he petitioned the ABCFM for service to the western Indians. James Orr was a mechanic from Hancock, New Hampshire, and was largely responsible for erecting the Mission's many buildings, most of which would be abandoned, when the Mission was relocated in 1829 to a place now known as Sallisaw, the county seat of Sequoyah County in Oklahoma.

Rev. Washburn was a strong, capable leader who fervently believed in the evangelization of the Indians and encouraged his teachers to work toward that end. The effects of alcohol on the Cherokees was another major concern of his, which he addressed by organizing a temperance society run entirely by Cherokees.

He was also concerned about his teaching staff. There had been illness among the missionaries almost continuously from the time they arrived. It was difficult for the New Englanders, in particular, to become acclimated. Malaria, then referred to as "intermittent fever," was common and often afflicted several people at one time. Many of the missionaries at the Dwight Mission requested releases from the station citing "ill health and the unsettled state of political affairs among the Cherokees."[8]

In 1839, one of the teacher/missionaries, Theresa Bissell, wrote: "The Missionaries are growing old and have almost worn themselves out in the service." By the standards of the time, they were not old, but the work, illness, and hardships had taken their toll.[9]

By 1841, Ellen Stetson, who had been in charge of the girls "out of school" and had been at the Dwight Mission since its inception in 1820, was one of those "worn out" missionaries and decided it was time to leave. Rev. Washburn, concerned about her replacement, wrote to the ABCFM "We can hardly expect one to be found whose qualifications shall be equal to Miss Stetson's, but we hope great pains will be taken to supply her place with some one whose worth may approximate as nearly as possible to Miss Stetson. It is desirable that her successor should be a lady of good health and under thirty years of age."

In an earlier letter, Rev. Washburn had spelled out, in detail, the qualities he believed a teacher should possess in working with the Cherokee children:

> A teacher should be conscientious. A sense of the preciousness of the charge committed to him, and his awful responsibility, should take an abiding, an almost overwhelming hold, on his mind. He must possess inexhaustible patience. He must have much mildness of disposition and manner. He must be persevering. He should have a good knowledge of the human heart. Every variety of character and temperament is often found in one school. How important then that the teacher be able to judge accurately to which variety each belongs. He must be industrious. He ought to regard industry as a Christian duty; to feel that every hour not usefully employed is sinfully thrown away.[10]

---

8     Campbell, O.B., *Mission to the Cherokees*, Metro Press, Oklahoma City, OK, 1971, pg. 69

9     Ibid

10    Washburn, Rev. Cephas, *Reminiscences of the Indians*, Presbyterian Committee of Publication, 1971

**Rev. Cephas Washburn**
Missionary, teacher, preacher, and
Evangelist who headed the Dwight
Mission for its first twenty years.

**Jacob Hitchcock**
One of the founders of Dwight Mission
and a force behind the institution for
nearly forty years—longer than any
other individual in the Mission's history.

Taken from *Mission to the Cherokees* by Campbell, 1971

In addition, Washburn stressed, "The major purpose of the establishment of the Mission is the salvation of the people." Hannah met these qualifications. She was certainly a lady of good health, although just over thirty years of age. She had been well-educated, had several years of teaching experience, and there was no doubt that she was dedicated to saving the souls of the Indians when she said in another of her letters, "Oh that it might please God to use me as an humble instrument of good to this benighted people."

The Dwight Mission was a "little village," situated on a hill, a half mile from a creek. The pleasant yard was surrounded by a rail fence, and every house was fenced off so that they had yards where the ladies had a few flowers, vines, and flowering shrubbery. The trees in the open campus were mostly locust, while in each house-yard, maple trees had been set out. There was a double log house with two rooms, each twenty feet square, with two stone chimneys, and a shingle roof. There was a passage ten feet wide through the middle, which was then occupied by Miss Stetson and the girls' school and would later be occupied by Hannah. The dining room and kitchen, built of hewn logs, was twenty-four by fifty-four feet in size and two stories high. One stone chimney provided two fireplaces, and there was a cellar twenty-four by thirty-four feet, walled and pointed with lime and mortar. In addition, there were two log cabins sixteen by twenty-one feet in size, a story-and-a-half high, made of hewn logs, chinked with stone, pointed with lime mortar, and whitewashed.

The boys' school was a two-story log house measuring eighteen by twenty-two feet with two rooms below and two above. One large stone chimney in the center furnished two fireplaces on each floor. There was a similar two-story house for Mr. Washburn. Mr. Gray, Jacob Hitchcock, and Mr. Orr were each provided with a story-and-a-half house with two fireplaces. A gallery eight feet wide ran across the front of each of these log houses. Two cabins were built for the laborers and another for an office.

According to a description written by Isaac Hitchcock, son of Jacob and Nancy (Brown) Hitchcock, many years after he had left the Mission, none of the buildings had glass windows. A small window, about two feet long, was made by cutting out one log. The opening was then provided with a wooden shutter. In addition to being the chief cook for the Mission, Isaac's father took care of two hundred to three hundred head of cattle and milked the cows.[11]

Soon after she arrived, Hannah penned a letter to her family in Union. Hannah wrote: "I found the buildings better than I had supposed log huts could be." There were about one hundred people at her first meal, and "when the sacred volume was read and all bowed around the tables to invoke the blessings of heaven, a tear stole down my cheek to think what self denial it must have cost the first missionaries to have got things going."[12]

Hannah had read the story of the Cherokee Indians who were forcibly removed from their homes in Georgia in 1834 and marched between six hundred and seven hundred miles to the Oklahoma Territory. Now, at the Dwight Mission, she was in a position to hear the story from the Cherokees themselves. She wrote:

> I have learned a number of facts relating to the manner in which the Cherokee Indians were compelled to leave the old nation (as they style it). They tell me they were driven from their homes on the point of the bayonet into the camps and they suffered from a great variety of contagious diseases such as measles, whooping cough etc., till in some families more than half their number died. Some fathers were commanded by the Georgia militia to leave the plow in the midst of the furrows &

11   Campell, Ibid (pg. 41)
12   Hannah Moore letter to Joanna Moore, April 4, 1842, OSV

hasten to the camps on pain of death without even permission to return to the house & notify the tender wife & loving children.

Approximately a month after her arrival, she composed a poem describing the plight of the Cherokees, which she mailed to her mother:

Mother! I'm here in the Cherokee Nation
With employment assigned at the Missionary Station
The work though important, but I wish to pursue
Though responsible and arduous to make my way through
There's a glorious prize at the end of the race
Which will more than repay all the toils of the place
And the souls of the heathen are worth far more
Than the wealth of the Indies or Emperor's store

The poor Aborigines robbed of their rights
Have traversed the wilderness in fugitive plights
They were driven from homes and the farms they did till
The white man said leave them, they are mine at my will.
And because the proud nation were stronger in arms
The civilized Indians must resign them their farms
The suffering and toils, which in journeying they passed
Caused thousands of Indians to breathe out their last

And then a good conscience will be prized far more
Than all the red Chieftains ever had in their store
And the conduct will be an even sale weighed
Without any regard to the color or shade

In her poem, Hannah obviously sympathized with the plight of the Indians, but she carefully avoided direct criticism of President Andrew Jackson. President Jackson defied the Supreme Court decision favoring the Five Tribes of Indians' right to keep their land in Georgia and made the decision to have the Cherokee and Choctaw Indians removed from their homes. On the other hand, the ABCFM took a strong stand that the Jackson and Van Buren administrations had criminally driven the five civilized tribes off their treaty lands, and doubted that the tribes could ever be successfully assimilated into the dominant white culture because of a profound distrust of it.[13]

---

13  McLoughlin, *Cherokees and Christianity*, pg. 39

Eager to begin working with the orphaned Indian children, Hannah readily entered into the daily routine at the Mission. During the summer, the bell (which was the size of a common wash bowl) rang at half-past six in the morning, when all the different families would surround an altar in each of the dwellings for morning prayers. At seven, the bell rang for breakfast, and everyone proceeded, "with much decorum," to the dining hall, where they found their seats with as little confusion as possible.[14]

Each of the six tables was covered with cotton sheeting, and the knives and forks were placed in order around them. The cups and saucers and earthen plates for the adults, and tin dippers and pewter plates for the children, were placed together at the head of each table. Hannah sat at the fifth table with two of the teachers and the Cherokee girls.

After all were seated, a signal for silence was given, a blessing implored, and the food eaten in a quiet atmosphere. Before leaving the table, a portion of scripture was read, accompanied by some practical observations, and then all knelt in prayer.

The breakfast invariably consisted of coffee, with a little milk and occasionally sugar or molasses, and corn bread, with meat that was always stewed. Benches surrounded the table as substitutes for chairs.

After breakfast the boys went to the fields, and the girls returned with Hannah to her house, where she instructed them in reading, spelling, arithmetic, history, and mental philosophy. They also learned to do various kinds of needlework, plain and ornamental, as well as spinning and weaving. The ladies of the Mission alternated duty, remaining in the dining room and kitchen to instruct the girls in the various branches of domestic affairs.

At nine o'clock the bell called the children from their labors to prepare for school. At twelve they were dismissed from study and allowed to amuse themselves until dinner. Boys and girls were not allowed to play together. At half-past twelve, dinner, consisting of some kind of meat, generally pork, sometimes beef, and occasionally venison; cold corn bread; and cold water was served.

After dinner, all went to their different employments until summoned to supper. This meal consisted of black tea, without sugar; hominy with a little milk; cold corn bread; and occasionally, butter. After supper and evening prayers, the children enjoyed some innocent recreation such as playing games, while the adults finished the work of the day. On Sunday the routine changed. During the fore-

---

14   *Dwight, A Brief History of Old Dwight Cherokee Mission 1820–1953*, Dwight Presbyterian Mission, Inc. 1954

noon, public worship was performed in English for the benefit of the Mission family. At the close of the services, the Cherokees arrived, and by the afternoon, the house was nearly filled with Indians who heard the services conducted in their native language. The sermon, however, was preached in English and interpreted to the people.

A month after Hannah's arrival, she, like her predecessors, had an attack of the "chill, fever and ague.... It appeared to me while the chill was one cold enough to freeze, (though a warm summer day) and when the fever came on it was warm enough, I thought, to burn up besides being in distressing pain." After about three or four weeks she regained her health, but what she didn't know was that she had contracted malaria, the cause of which was unknown at the time, and that she would have recurrent attacks the rest of her life.

After five months Hannah had already made an impression on the Mission fathers regarding her teaching methods. She reported to Reverend Greene that she was surprised to learn that after two or three terms with another teacher, her students could neither add nor subtract.

> On a close survey, I found their learning much more superficial than I at first imagined. When questioning whether they understood their sums they would frequently answer in the affirmative, but when asked to explain it, they could not do it in any good degree. I thought it necessary to make allowances because they were not so well versed in the English language.
>
> Still, I regret to say, I had taught near three months and heard their daily recitation to the more obtuse sections in fractions and was searching for a reason why they should come to me so often to have it explained notwithstanding I had tried so much to make it plain and intelligible by having them count corns and divide potatoes into fractional parts thinking, without fail, I should bring it to their capacity by such processes, when it occurred to my mind that there must be some deficiency in the elementary parts and set them very simple sums in addition. Not one of them could do them having never been taught to add on their slates.
>
> I knew my scholars in New England understood arithmetic better, but did not know anyone could go so far in mental arithmetic and not understand the simplest parts. I attributed the problem to the (previous) mode of teaching rather than any natural or mental deficiency in the pupils.

The classes in history and mental philosophy recited very well, better than in some schools in Connecticut. I had some very good readers and was pleased with the proficiency made in that branch.

Some ladies who had never been taught writing learned a good hand so as to be able to write letters home and compositions. I think in all my teaching, at the best, it is not common to find scholars who learn writing equally well in the same length of time.

The most prominent defect in their letters and composition was bad spelling. This I found difficult to correct though I tried various modes. One of the best of which, I think, was to read the composition before the school and when I came to a misspelt word, read it as it was written and then ask the class how it should be spelled and give the delimitation. This left an impression likely to be permanent while a blush would sometimes betray the writer whose name I did not disclose.[15]

A letter written by Hannah to her mother and sisters in Union, Connecticut contains examples of her students' handwriting and, in one case, a wry sense of humor.

To Miss Amy Moore

I am a Cherokee girl at Dwight and attending school. Your sister requested me to write you. I suppose her object was to let you know that Indian girls could learn to write and distinguish peas, and beans, from potatoes and pumpkins just as well as white girls.

---

15     Hannah Moore to Rev. Mr. Green, March 30, 1842

I should like for you to write me.

Apr. 5, 1842

P.S. There are a great many white people in this country that can neither read nor write, <u>I pity them</u>.

Rutha L. Wilson

Hannah had as many as forty-five children, mostly girls, and just when she
felt she was making progress, she was asked to give up the school to Mrs. Day,
who was also a teacher there. "I acknowledge it was repugnant to my feelings
to give them up so soon after becoming acquainted with the extent of their
requirements."

She obviously made her feelings known, as we learn from a letter written by
Mr. Hitchcock. He writes that, "rather than have any unpleasant feelings, we con-
sented that she should keep the school until the first of February."

From all reports, Miss Stetson, whom Hannah replaced, was an excellent
teacher, however, she was from the "old school," where women were expected to
defer to the male authority figure. Hannah, on the other hand, was not afraid to
voice her opinions or take a firm stand which, as we will see, was not always well
received:

> I knew from personal conversation with my pupils that some of them
> were interested about the salvation of their souls so much so as to entreat
> an interest in my prayers in their behalf. I took an early opportunity to
> mention the favorable indications to Mr. Hitchcock. He said the pupils
> were easily excited and it was easy to work up their feelings to a certain
> pitch and added he should be very sorry to have a zealous Methodist
> come among them now, adding we have no minister and I am not look-
> ing for a revival. I came home with sad feelings and committed my way
> to the Lord, feeling I could not have the cooperation of the mission
> family in promoting a revival.[16]

---

16   Hannah Moore to Rev. David Green, March 30, 1842, ABCFM

It appears, however, that Mr. Hitchcock changed his mind and accepted some of the Cherokees into the Christian fellowship prior to Rev. Willey's arrival. This prompted Hannah to write another letter to the Mission Board criticizing Hitchcock, stating that it was her impression that none of the Cherokee Indians who wished to become Christian could take that step without an ordained minister's authority, and that Mr. Hitchcock, therefore, had acted improperly. She wrote, "The world is to be converted by the preaching of the gospel, which seemed to me to imply a doubt whether these souls would be converted here where we have no pastor or stated preaching."[17]

Undeterred, she continued working towards her goal of "saving souls," with the hope that a minister would soon arrive who could confirm her efforts. She told her students, "I did not leave my home and friends and come out here merely to teach the sciences or how to work, but I had another object in view even the salvation of their immortal souls and would direct them to the Lamb of God."[18]

After her first year at the Dwight Mission, Hannah had her first real horseback riding excursion, which she described in a letter home. It should be noted that she would have been riding sidesaddle since it was not considered ladylike to ride astride:

> I rode twenty miles without alighting, through creeks and rivers without bridges, which was rather fatiguing though I was delighted with the foreign and romantic scenery. After visiting a few days at Fairfield, we set out on a cold, stormy morning in February on horseback ... over some frightful precipices, I once should have thought impassable on horseback. Then we would descend and enter a ravine and then a forest so dense as to render it necessary to guard my bonnet or leave it among the boughs. When we reached the Illinois (River) near Park Hill, I found a larger river than any we had forded—so deep I thought my horse literally swam through. Doctor Butler said he thought my head swam. I told (him) I was sure it was heavy enough to sink; this gave us such a cheer we passed over safe.[19]

This was the first indication of Hannah's sense of humor, which in her missionary zeal and dedication to teaching and the conversion of the native children to Christianity, was not apparent in her letters.

---

17   Ibid
18   Hannah Moore to Rev. David Green, August 4, 1842, ABCFM
19   Hannah Moore to Rev. David Green, September 10, 1844, ABCFM

It was at Park Hill, near the border of Texas, that she met John Ross, the chief of the Cherokee Nation. In appearance he was a white man, being only one-eighth Cherokee, but he exerted great influence over the full-blooded members of the Cherokee Nation. It was Ross who resisted the Federal Indian Removal policy for nearly ten years and ultimately led his people on the long and painful trek to Oklahoma. Hannah frequently vacationed with members of Ross's extended family and that of his chief associate, Joseph Lowery.

Understanding the value of education, Ross was instrumental in the establishment of the missionary schools in his territory, and he did

**Chief John Ross**
Courtesy of Philbrook Museum
of Art, Tulsa, Oklahoma

everything he could to help the missionaries. He strongly supported the Dwight Mission's teaching of mechanical training for the boys and homemaking skills for the girls.

When it became apparent that there were not enough people to manage both boys and girls adequately, Ross's advice was "You had better not take boys unless you have someone to take care of them."

Hannah obviously thought differently. Mr. Hitchcock, in a letter to the ABCFM, referred to the situation saying:

> I do not think anyone doubts Mr. Day's willingness to take charge of the boys in school and out, but no one thinks it advisable, under existing circumstances, unless it is Miss Moore. She has appeared to think that the more children we get together the better, and has said that carrying on the farm and attending to domestic labors indoors and out was not missionary labor.[20]

There was no doubt in Hannah's mind that the work of the farm and domestic labors should be done by someone other than the teachers, and that the first priority should be the education of both boys and girls.

---

20   Jacob Hitchcock to Rev. David Green July 17, 1844, ABCFM

In 1844, three years after Hannah's arrival, Jacob Hitchcock, superintendent of the Dwight Mission, was requested to make a report to the ABCFM regarding the status of the Mission. He responded:

> The scholars gathered around us are almost always rude and uncultivated both in mind and morals. Their minds are generally low and groveling, rising but little above the ground upon which they tread. What shall I eat and drink and wherewithal shall I amuse myself seem to be the height of their inquiries. Their moral sense is very obtuse and selfishness seem(s) the supreme law of their actions. At home they are seldom subject to parental authority and know little restraint but what exists in the nature of things around them. Hence their habits are bad. They are addicted to lying and deception of almost every species such is the general character of those received under our care.
>
> To change this character from what it is to what it ought to be, is the great object of our efforts. To elevate the mind—give them a thorough knowledge of the first principles of science—to improve their habits—cultivate their morals and point them to the Lamb of God that taketh away the sins of the world, are the objects of which we aim. To some, our efforts are abundantly blessed in the improvement of their habits—the elevation of their minds the reforming of their morals, and to some, we trust, the salvation of their souls; while to others every effort is but as water spilt on the ground.[21]

After such a dismal picture, it would seem there wasn't much hope for improvement, but surprisingly, he concluded that "most of the scholars have made decidedly good proficiency in their studies, including reading, writing, spelling, arithmetic, grammar, history, 'Watts on the Mind' and natural philosophy." He stopped short of giving the teachers credit for the progress made.

The Dwight Mission had not had a minister for five years when Rev. Willey arrived in 1845. Apparently he was not well-received by Jacob Hitchcock and perhaps others. In a letter to Reverend Green, Secretary of the Mission Board, Kellogg Day, one of the teachers, aired his opinion of Mr. Willey:

---

21   Ibid

**Early School Building constructed of logs at the Dwight Mission, 1829**

**Rev. Worcester Willey, Missionary at Dwight from 1845 until after the Civil War.**

Taken from *Mission to the Cherokees* by Campbell, 1971

Mr. Willey has said that the school is unpopular among the Cherokees. Now if the school is justly unpopular I certainly could not think it my duty to continue in it any longer. To the contrary there has been a constant press of scholars and applicants from some of the highest officers of the Cherokee nation. Again, I have the pleasure of knowing that some who have enjoyed the privileges of the school speak of it in terms of the highest confidence. But while all this is true, some have undoubtedly been disaffected, because their children were not received into school, some because they were rejected after a few months' trial— some because we do not take boys—some because we do not live to suit them—and some, no doubt, because they did not like the management of the teachers.

James Orr, who by this time had been made Superintendent of Secular Affairs, wrote to the ABCFM in support of Rev. Willey, saying he hoped what he had to say would go no further, or it would "bring about more and worse difficulties." He wrote, "I have known that ever since Mr. Willey came here there had existed unpleasant feelings on the part of Mr. Hitchcock but was not fully aware of the extent of his feelings.... A word or two about Mr. Willey. He has his peculiarities, some of which are a little troublesome, but he is a good man and perhaps doing more good than all the rest of us."[22]

---

22    James Orr to Rev. David Green, May 10, 1847, ABCFM

Hannah strongly supported Rev. Willey. She felt that he was the answer to her prayers, saying: "I find my anticipation of a good preacher and faithful missionary realized in Mr. Willey and return thanks to your Board for sending us the very one needed." She had, at last, found someone who supported her ideas regarding the operation of the Mission and said, "I have my fears that the same who disapprove of my labors, will of his." This undoubtedly is a reference to her frequent disagreements with Jacob Hitchcock. In a later letter she wrote, "Mr. Willey is taking the same ground with regard to seeking the good of the Indians, rather than secure the approbation of the Mission family."

In the fall of 1845, Mr. and Mrs. Day announced their intention to leave the station due to a long series of health problems. Having confidence in Hannah's abilities, Mr. Day asked her to take charge of the school until the new teacher arrived, an offer she willingly accepted.

It was about this time that she again became ill and wrote: "Although I had no assistant, the pupils, it seemed, tried to outdo each other in their attention to me and often would solicit the priviledge (sic) of staying out of school to attend on me. I gradually recovered my health which is pretty good still, though not as it was when I commenced my labor at this station."

At the close of the term, one of the parents sent a horse so that she could go to some of her students' homes.

> I met a cordial reception and received all the attention and respect, which seemed in their power to bestow. Notwithstanding all this my heart was pained at the supineness of parents and indolence of the children. I regret to say almost all had slaves to perform all their laborious work while they, with folded hands, idly sat without any employment in their houses.
>
> The children thus early accustomed to have a slave to fan them when they sleep and wait on and carry them when awake, early imbibe habits which need a large share of wisdom joined with prudence and dexterity to eradicate. This seems to me the grand secret of the imbecility of their minds [and explains] why they do not expand faster.[23]

Up to this point, Hannah had not seen how the Cherokees used their black slaves, nor had she seen the effect it had on the Indian families. This experience solidified her belief: "I feel confident if slavery could be done away with then would they make far greater progress in the arts and sciences."

---

23    Hannah Moore to Rev. David Green, September 10, 1844, ABCFM

It was not just the fact that the Cherokees had slaves that opened Hannah's eyes; she also witnessed the traditional Green Corn dance, a fertility ceremony:

> They had a green corn dance while I was with them. Built a large fire & danced around it, hold of hand, & roasted their corn baked their hough cake in the woods. But Oh! their Ball play, and Saturday night dances are shocking to humanity. They play on a wager staking their property for the success of a useless game of running.[24]

Perhaps more disturbing than the actual ceremony, was the fact that the night dances carried over to Sunday, thus violating or "breaking" the Sabbath. When she realized that there would be another corn dance the following Saturday, she decided to leave and had not gone far when she and her guide were overtaken:

> We had not proceeded far before a company of ballplayers overtook us riding full speed whiskey bottles hanging at their sides. Though a great many females attend these plays my guide knew I did not wish for a moment to look on a scene so disgusting to refinement as Indians running in a state of nudity. When we came nearer the scene he halted & I dare not raise my eyes to look forward till we turned from the road into a grove of Sycamores so thick as entirely to conceal them from our view & we passed secure, & reached home in safety.[25]

Whether other female missionaries had been invited to stay with Cherokee families for a two-week period is not known, but it can be assumed that Hannah had earned their respect and confidence. On the other hand, neither their confidence nor the confidence she enjoyed from the ABCFM was shared by Jacob Hitchcock. Hitchcock wrote to Rev. David Green on several occasions complaining about Hannah's unwillingness to accept authority. He wrote: "She was too wise, selfconfident, selfwilled, and selfconceited to take advice sometimes." He felt there was a need for "a different person to take charge of the girls out of school." He went on to say that "it was impossible to represent things on paper as they really are; and I will not attempt it. I often wish you could see with your own eyes, and then you would be prepared to act."

Hannah continued to report to the ABCFM, complaining about Hitchcock's demands regarding her record-keeping, which was another bone of contention. Apparently Hitchcock was keeping track of what Hannah was receiving and com-

---

24   Ibid

25   Ibid

paring his records with hers so that she was constantly having to defend herself. She recounted one incident in particular that raised her hackles when she realized her accounts were being charged with things she never received:

> A piece of patchwork and bottle of indelible ink was invoiced to me & I had no further intelligence of them. One time a black bonnet which I neither sent for or needed came. I proposed selling it as an opportunity presented, but objections were made & Mrs. Hitchcock, who still wears it, found an occasion to wear it on the death of her daughter.

If Hitchcock implied that Hannah was spending money on herself, she made it quite clear that that was not the case.

> I am still wearing the same bonnet I brought with me. The same dilapidated curtains hang at the windows now which I found when I came & I have purchased only two articles of household or cabinet furniture, a bureau & table, but I paid for them together with the additional expense of them here in money presented by my Sister, now dead, before I left my father's house, being the avails of a gold necklace, I would not receive to wear though I wish to have something I could daily use & behold as a memorial of her.

While Hannah was vacationing with the Cherokee families, Hitchcock formally demanded that Hannah be reassigned.

> We may almost as well be without a school as to have Miss Moore teach it. However well she may have done in N. England, she is not a suitable person for this school, neither is she a suitable person to take charge of the girls out of school. And I am fully convinced that the interest of the Mission and the school require that another person be provided as soon as convenient to take her place.[26]

Upon her return to the Dwight Mission, she learned that arrangements had been made for her transfer to the Choctaw Mission near the border of Texas. She wrote to the Mission Board: "If I have erred in exhibiting too much spirit of censorship, pardon me. Since I have given up my own dear parents, I have addressed you in childlike simplicity as a parent who would use your influence to set things right." Knowing Hannah's propensity to jump into the fray, her reference to "childlike simplicity," must have raised the eyebrows of the ABCFM.

---

26   Jacob Hitchcock to Rev. David Greene, October 16, 1845, ABCFM

Rev. Green, in a letter addressed to Hannah and dated November 5, 1845, wrote: "Within the last few months I learn that your associates in the missionary work think that your manner of viewing things generally, especially in relation to teaching and managing the pupils, is not adapted to render you useful, or to promote the best interests of the school." There was also a reference to her eyes: "They think that interposes an obstacle in the way of your success in your labors."

About a month later she replied, in a letter dated December 14, 1845, that her eyesight was adequate and had never been considered a drawback by her associates. She said she frequently stayed up late doing fine sewing and writing letters by candlelight.

Although she was initially upset when she was transferred to Mt. Pleasant, an American Board station 130 miles south in the Choctaw Nation near the site of present-day Caney, Oklahoma, she found that the Choctaws were

> more ready to receive the truth in the love of it than the Cherokees. My school, though very little advanced in comparison with the one at Dwight is notwithstanding, very pleasant and interesting considering they all speak the Indian dialect and are only in the rudiments of English education. With these embarrassments in view I think they advance as rapidly as could be expected. Indeed, it appears some of the full-blooded Indians are more docile and studious than the mixed races.[27]

While at the Choctaw Mission an outbreak of a deadly fever epidemic claimed the lives of some of Hannah's pupils and left others blinded by its symptoms. Hannah was afflicted as well and lost the sight in her left eye as a result.

Having observed the practice of slavery among the Cherokees, Hannah was now challenged by a new law regarding the activities of missionaries which made it "unlawful for any person or persons whatever, to teach any free negro or negroes not of Cherokee blood, or any slave belonging to any citizen or citizens of the nation, to read or write." She was compelled to inform the American Board of her views in a letter dated 16 January 1847:

> I have one prominent objection, however, to laboring among the Indians in this section of the country which is their connection with slaves and the severe laws that are passed by them stating that missionaries must forfeit their privilege of remaining in the country by even teaching a slave in the Sabbath School. Indeed, I do not well know how to put up

---

27    Hannah Moore to Rev. Daniel Green dated January 16, 1847, ABCFM

with some of the new laws which are more intolerable than the former ones in protecting slavery and its concomitant evils. It seems to me most prudent to observe silence for the most part among slaveholders and this I have practiced.[28]

While she may have observed silence among slaveholders, that obviously didn't apply to the children of slaveholders.

On looking over my list of pupils which I have taught during these six years, since on Mission ground, I find 36 were children of slaveholders & doubtless others of whom I am uninformed; four of them being orphans who inherited slaves, being thus literally slaveholders.

To such I have not hesitated to speak of the evils of the system, & tell them plainly that God was no respecter of one more than another. His holy word, declaring that in every nation he that feareth God & worketh righteousness is accepted, rendering it evident that one person was as good as another if his conduct was such, the action being the surest criterion to prove one better than another, & that the veriest slave might, by obeying from the heart declaring that in every nation he that feareth God & worketh righteousness is accepted, rendering it evident that one person was as good as another if the commands of God, prove himself better than his master & thus be prepared for a state of felicity hereafter which his early master would come short of. And I have, in conversing with slaves, observed much caution, even admonishing them to submit to every ordinance of man for the Lord's sake & look for their reward in a better & happier state of existence.[29]

After receiving word that her father's health was declining, she requested permission to return to Connecticut during the summer. She also needed time to recover from her most recent illness. "It was necessary, greatly to my sorrow, to give up reading, and study of all kinds, even the Bible," because of weakened eyesight.

Referring them to Rev. Samuel Worcester, who was superintendent of the Cherokee Mission and Rev. W. Willey, she wrote:

Ask them if they ever saw me in a passion or fretful and satisfy yourself. For all your Christian admonitions and counsels and smiting, reproofs and buffetings, I now thank you. I cannot say, as did our Saviour when

---

28    Ibid
29    Ibid

they took up the stones to stone Him, "for which of my good works do you stone me, for mine have all been imperfect."

Although Hannah enjoyed working with the Choctaw Indian children, she could not, in good conscience, continue as long as the ABCFM would not take a stand against slavery. In a March 19, 1847 letter, Rev. Green agreed that her return to the Choctaw Nation would not be feasible.

In a letter to Rev. Green dated June 11, 1847, she again refers to the slavery question: "And then there was the subject of slavery which I am informed is about to cause a separation between the ABCFM and those Indian Missions connected with it & is even now causing the removal of some of its Missionaries to other fields of labor."

His reply finalized Hannah's decision regarding her future:

I can appreciate your feelings in the dislike you express of laboring in a country where slavery is maintained. There must be much that is painful and disheartening in the scenes which such a state of things presents. But I suppose that we must have some patience with these evils which we cannot at once correct, though they offend & grieve us. God's forbearance is far greater than ours, though those evils are far more offensive to him.

She was not one to sit back and let things take their course when it came to the leadership and organization of the Dwight Mission and obviously stepped on some toes along the way. She indicated as much when, in June 1849, she wrote to Rev. Green from Willington, Connecticut, saying: "Were I again to enter a mission field, it would be my choice to labor where I should be most useful rather than where I should be most popular."

It is also appears that she was sharply criticized by someone at the Choctaw Mission:

You seem to overlook every sacrifice I have made for missions and to be harping on my besetting sins of Anger which, by the grace of God, I doubt not I shall entirely overcome, at least so as to obey the injunction, "Be ye angry and sin not." You ask me to "select some brother in the Choctaw Mission in whom I have the most confidence and inquire of him whether I was not culpable both with tongue and pen." There is no living Missionary in whom I have more confidence than Brother Byington in the Choctaw Mission.

Rev. Green urged her to be patient, but that was something Hannah wasn't willing or even able to do. The slavery issue would, in the final analysis, determine Hannah's future. As the year of her convalescence drew to a close, she was faced with some difficult decisions, but she eventually decided that she wanted to spend the rest of her life in the service of the ABCFM. She wrote:

> I feel entirely willing to go under the patronage of the Board to any Island of the Sea, to the further coast of Asia, or the burning sands of Africa. I leave this fair heritage to someone who would not dare venture so far among cruel barbarians. I would fain cherish the fond hope of being a missionary to the end of my life, whether long or short. To be a good and successful missionary seems to me the acme of human felicity, the highest fruition of my earthly hopes and the employment seems nearest allied to that of angels and of our blessed Savior on earth. But whatever the will of God may be respecting me, may I cheerfully submit resigning myself to him in well doing as to a faithful Creator who surely will do right.

The slavery question and the fact that the American Board of Foreign Commissioners had not fully supported her activities at the Dwight Mission led Hannah to ally herself with a new Society, which had just been organized in 1846. When the American Missionary Society (AMS) announced its devotion to the abolition of slavery by peaceful means, Hannah switched her allegiance and applied to the AMS for a position "anywhere."

Hannah had been teaching school in Pulaski, New York, for two years (1848–1850) when she asked Rev. Thomas Salmon, the minister at the Congregational Church, for a character reference to support her application to the AMS. It may have been at this time that Hannah changed the spelling of her surname to "More," as this is the spelling Rev. Salmon used in his letter quoted below.

Hannah's decision to go abroad may have been furthered by Rev. Salmon, since he had been a missionary in India and Ceylon for nearly twenty years, where he assisted in translating the Bible into fourteen languages. His letter, dated November 15, 1850, follows:

Pulaski, Oswego Co., N.Y.
15 Nov. 1850

The Secretaries
American Miss. Society

Dear Sirs,

Miss H. More has resided in this neigh-
borhood for some two years. I believe
that she is unusually respected and I
know that she is much beloved as a Sister
and an active Christian by all the members of our church and society who are
acquainted with her. We trust and pray
that the divine providence may open a
way for the employment of her talents
in the promotion of the Saviour's glory.
Your brother and friend in the gospel of
our Lord.

Thomas Salmon, Pastor—1st Cong. Ch.
Congregational Church, Pulaski, New York

**Congregational Church, Pulaski, NY**
Taken from "*Grip's*" *Historical Souvenir
of Pulaski*, 1902

# Chapter Four: "The Return of the Amistad"

The now-famous overthrow of the *Amistad* occurred while Hannah was living and working in the Oklahoma Territory. News was slow to travel to the Oklahoma Territory—letters would take at least a month to arrive from New York—so it is not known whether Hannah heard about the plight of the Africans aboard the *Amistad*. If she had, she probably would have mentioned it in her letters to her family or to the ABCFM, since she had made it clear to those with whom she worked that she was an abolitionist and would, therefore, have been sympathetic to the cause of the Africans. Little did she realize that in a few years, she would come to know some of these men and women personally and learn what happened to them once they were freed.

The following account of the *Amistad* events was related by Hannah in a letter she wrote to Mr. Harned on October 12, 1852, while working and living in Africa:

> These captives were stolen from their homes and transported to the West Indies for bond Slaves! Some of them were taken in war, others were sold for debt or by their fond parents with the hope of redeeming them. They were seized on from different parts of the country. Some were taken far away in the interior, where they never had heard, so as to understand, about the mighty waters of the broad Atlantic. Imagine then the surprise of Sinque & Posey when, for the first time, they beheld the proud waves of the Ocean foaming and breaking at their feet. Sinque, a prince, & Alick (as we call him), the head man of the town, both taken in war and conveyed, or rather, driven, manacled on the trackless Ocean.
>
> Sinque tried various ways to animate and keep up the depressed spirits of his countrymen. I will give you part of the first speech he made on deck, in his native dialect, which the people do not love to spoil by translating into English. "Brothers, we are from the same coun-

try. Keep up your spirits. These sad Faces bode no good for us freeborn Mendingoes. Is not ours a bold warlike nation? We may be somebody, who knows, but we may be freemen yet. Anyhow, let us make the best of our condition."

They tell me they were on the Ocean 3-1/2 months in reaching Cuba for which there seems to be no just cause aside from their anchoring & circuitous meandering course to elude the search of an English Man of War. It should be remembered they were heathen and reckoned their time only by moons and are very liable to make errors in their calculations.

At Havanna (sic) they passed ten days & were disposed of in a Slave Market to different purchasers—some from Brazil, some from Jamaica and different places. This being the case, they were shipped on the Brig Amistad for their several places of destination. And here, for the first time, they saw Sarah Margru & Maria. It seems they crossed the Ocean in different Vessels. About 25 miles from Havanna they discovered a Frigate pursuing them and landed to elude their pursuit. They were marched into the bush till in sight of Havanna. Next they were dressed like Sailors & taken on board the Amistad. Well they might feel sad, but who can portray the depth of their misery when they found themselves bond men & women in a strange land, far removed from all they valued on earth—torn from the bosom of their parents, their depths of the ocean and they could not remember particulars now and I need not ask them. But this they remember, that their scanty allowance of food was half a tumbler of water per day for each person & half a plantain per meal. They know not why, but this was all the Captain of the Amistad allowed them for a long time.

Much more honorable it would be to die fighting for life than tamely submit to be slaughtered for Cannibals to feast on, they all assented, or as the people here say, all had one word WAR!! & war immediately. At a signal, understood by none but themselves, all were ready. Though they had searched the day previous for arms and found none, providentially, at this juncture, a box of knives and cutlasses were found in the hold so that all might be armed. Sinque commenced the attack by throwing a billet of wood at the Cook. Though it was his death wound, he screamed so as to alarm all on board the ship. Some of the sailors jumped overboard and were never heard of after. The Captain soon made his appearance armed with deadly weapons. At sight of him, many of the affrighted Slaves leaped overboard, but still held on to the mouldings of the ship. Again, all the eloquence of Sinque was needed. He exclaimed, "Oh! My People! Why are you so foolish! Do not throw away your lives! Come back and quit yourselves like men! You can but die in doing this & if you commit yourselves to the deep, death is inevitable—the Sea monster's will devour you! Come back, my brethren, my brave countrymen!" At this they came back.

The Captain had been kept at bay during this speech though he understood not a word of it. The next proposition was who shall fight the Captain. As no one dared approach him singly they agreed to surround him in the form of a phalanx well knowing, though valiant, he could not disarm or kill them all at one single stroke. He slew only one ere his head was dissevered and his mangled corpse thrown into the depth of the Sea. Then the air and the ocean reverberated with the yells and frantic dances of a savage clan. Some of them were for putting their Masters to death, but they said let us shed no unnecessary blood. We can secure them with chains which, accordingly, they did—the Captain and Cook being the only ones they put to death in capturing the Amistad & its officers & their masters or owners.

As they knew nothing about steering a ship they wished to spare the Mate & seaman to convey them back to their native shore, to the fond arms of their parents, and the homes made desolate by their absence. The direction they knew not save that their native land lay towards the rising Sun & in that direction they bade Master, the helmsman, to steer as they knew nothing about navigation, even the Mariner's compass was an insoluble mystery to them. How then could they know anything of the barometer, or quadrant, or have any data by which they might know where on the seas they might be. In this dilemma, the Master took every opportunity to sail towards Spain, the land of his nativity. This he could accomplish in cloudy weather and during the night. Of the north star they knew nothing, as it is but seldom seen here under the equator. Chronometers, watches & clocks were mere playthings to their beclouded minds. The sun and moon were their only time pieces. In this way, they made very slow progress & their suffering for water and suitable food was extreme. They had no water on board. When it rained they caught all the water they could & even wrung the Sails to allay their intolerable thirst. They were obliged to cook their food in and drink seawater. In this extremity, nine of their number died.

They hailed a French vessel and gave Spanish Doubloons. They were in a sad condition and terrible the conflict in their dark minds when they beheld New York City with its lofty spires peering in view. They dared not land for fear of being put to some horrid death for murdering the Captain and cook, so they find themselves again on the trackless ocean. Soon they approached New Haven and anchored. Soon rumor is afloat that a strange vessel is there hoping, yet fearing, to get water. They pay largely for a little fruit. Montes (the Captain) induced them to stop by telling them the Slaves' friends lived there.

Still they were apprehensive of the results, but rather than perish for water, ventured to make the experiment, when lo! they were seized for mutiny and cast into prison and various trials awaited them. Many were intent on making bondage for life their inevitable destiny. But they tell me the God of heaven fought for them for the judge who was about to condemn them was found dead in his bed the following morning. The Great Judge sent in his place a venerable gray haired man to vindicate their cause.

Long live the memory of John Q. Adams, their eloquent advocate. He gained for them their cause and declared they were well entitled to freedom and its privileges. After six months imprisonment at New Haven they were set at liberty. The Spaniards, in vain, tried to take them away by force. The Captain of one of their vessels was drowned in returning to his ship.

When they met on the Amistad their number was 54. They tell me 10 died on the passage to New Haven which was performed in two & one half months. Four died while they were undergoing their trials at New Haven.

The Lord raised up friends through the agency of your Association, who returned them to their native country with Missionaries to instruct them in Christianity & all that can elevate & refine a barbarous & savage people.

The Amistad Committee, later to become the American Missionary Association (AMA), organized a series of appeals to local churches where the Africans told their stories and demonstrated the results of their education and conversion to Christianity in an effort to raise money to buy the Africans' passage back to Africa. After approximately two years, they managed to raise $1,840 and chartered the barque, *Gentleman,* to make the return voyage in November of 1841.

The abolitionists who had allied themselves with the former African prisoners envisioned not just the abolition of slavery in the United States as well as the Atlantic slave trade, but also sought to transform African society by sending Christian missionaries to Africa. Quoting from Marie Cable's *Black Odyssey*:

> To find missionaries who were willing to go to West Africa was something like recruiting astronauts today, but more difficult. They had to be not only intelligent, level-headed, resourceful, and courageous to the point of recklessness, but impeccable Christians as well; furthermore they had to choose between leaving their families for a period of years or taking them along into what was certainly no exaggeration to term the jaws of death.

Lewis Tappan, an abolitionist and responsible for convincing John Quincy Adams to defend the captives, organized the Amistad Committee referred to above. Tappan made every effort to recruit capable clergymen with whom he was acquainted, but none of them were willing to leave their parishes. He was much relieved when he received a letter of application from William Raymond who stated his belief that he had been called by God to go to Western Africa.

Ever skeptical, Tappan decided to hire Raymond to teach the Africans who were then living in Farmington, Connecticut, and then asked members of the Amistad Committee to observe Raymond. One member wrote: "I don't think Raymond is the man to take charge." No reason was given, at the time.

Tappan was convinced that time had run out and that the Amistad people must go home as soon as arrangements could be made. He finally decided to send Raymond and two more missionaries, who had stepped forward to join Raymond even though he wasn't completely persuaded of Raymond's qualifications. James Steele, a former student at Oberlin, was highly recommended by his teachers. Tappan was glad to learn that he understood how to run a printing press, which the committee planned to send along for printing tracts that were to be distributed to the "heathen" as soon as they were able to read. Henry Wilson, a West Indian, and his wife, Tamar, a former Hartford servant girl whose employer assured the committee that her character was above reproach, completed the group.

Although they were warmly welcomed upon their arrival in Freetown, Sierra Leone, grim news awaited them. The Amistad captives learned that warring tribes had wiped out their villages and their families. But because the missionaries had been instructed to locate the Mission in the Mendi country, the home of most of the Amistad Africans, they were determined to explore the region which was in the interior about three or four days journey from Freetown. Steele left immediately to explore that region. When he found that the land was low, swampy, and very unhealthy, and that the Mendi chiefs were at war with each other and extremely hostile to the proposed missionary enterprise, the missionaries had to abandon the idea of locating there.

The Mission was temporarily established at York, about twenty-five miles south of Freetown, and three years later, in 1844, moved to Kaw-Mendi, which was in the Sherbro country, about 150 miles southeast of Sierra Leone and approximately 40 miles from the coast.

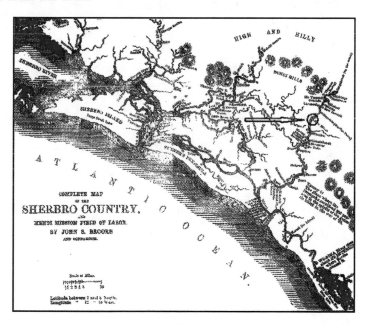

**The Kaw Mendi Mission was located 30 miles inland on the large island of Sherbro, 120 miles south of Freetown, and is marked by a circle and an arrow.**

Taken from "The Palm Land," by George Thompson

**Map of Sierra Leone, West Africa as of 2006**
Taken from Lonely Planet Publications, Oakland, CA

At the time of the relocation to Kaw Mendi, the only members of the original company remaining were Mr. and Mrs. Raymond and six of the Mendians including Sarah Kinson (Mar-gru), George Lewis (Ka-li), Lewis Johnson (Kinna), Alexander Posey (Fa-ban-na), Marie (The-me), and Charlotte (Keh-ne).

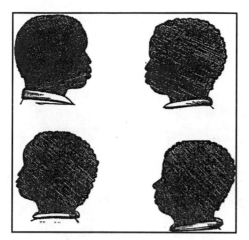

Silhouettes and information extracted from
Barber's *History of the Amistad Captives*
published in 1840

Top left: Ka-li (George Lewis) 4 ft. 3"—a small boy, with a large head, flat and broad nose, stout build. His parents were living; he had a sister and brother. He was stolen when in the street, and was about a month in traveling to Lomboko.

Top right: Mar-gru (Sarah Kinson) 4 ft. 3"— her parents were living; she had four sisters and two brothers. She was pawned by her father for a debt, which being unpaid, she was sold into slavery.

Bottom left: Ka-gne (Charlotte) She counts consecutively in Mendi like Kwong. Her parents were living. She had four brothers and four sisters.

Bottom right: Te-me (Maria) lived with her mother and brother and sister. Her father was dead. A party of men broke into their house and made them prisoners. She never saw her mother or brother again.

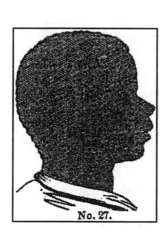

Fa-ban-na
Alexander Posey

He had two wives and one child
He was taken prisoner and sold twice

Sarah (Margru) Kinson
Age 10
Courtesey of Beinike Library, Yale University

Margru, or Sarah Kinson, the anglicized name given her by the abolitionists in Connecticut as a symbol of her free status, was destined to play an important role in the establishment of the Kaw Mendi Mission. An undated phrenological[30] study conducted prior to her return to Africa follows.

> She has a large head and a strong physical constitution, and is capable of putting forth and sustaining long continued vigorous bodily and mental effort. Her moral and intellectual organs, as a class, predominate over the animal propensities. She is honest and cautious in character and motive, and decidedly friendly and benevolent in disposition. She is very fond of children; is not inclined to contention or unusual irritability. She is very independent in her spirit and is not easily subjugated to the control of others, especially if potential measures are employed to affect it. I should judge that she could hardly be made a slave. Her spirit would rebel and struggle for emancipation.
>
> She is not shy nor cunning, though she is highly cautious and careful of consequences, yet frank in the expression of her opinions. She is decidedly firm in her feelings and opinions and may sometimes be willful and too independent, but an address to her large benevolence, prudence, justice and love of approbation, judiciously administered, will generally allay these asperities of character and mould her disposition and conduct. She is saving, economical, neat, fond of ornament and display, quite ingenious, initiative, and intelligent mechanically.
>
> She has an intelligent and naturally comprehensive mind, and is capable of gaining and retaining education. She has a good memory of what she sees and hears, requests but one telling to recollect a fact or process and readily becomes familiar with the manner and customs of those with whom she is brought in contact. She is thorough in whatever she engages and naturally industrious and efficient.
>
> If she were educated she would have unusual grasp of mind and power to stamp her character on, and exert influence over others. She is elevated in her feelings and decidedly ambitious to excel and gain the good will of the better class of minds.

---

30   Phrenology—the practice of studying character and mental capacity from the conformation of the skull. It never achieved the status of an accredited science.

She is buoyant, cheerful and sportive in her disposition, and warmly attached to friends and home. She is diffident among strangers, but soon gains her equilibrium and has a good share of confidence. She never wastes time nor energy, is patient, constant and evangelic and can be relied upon.

It was reported that when Sarah read the report she laughed heartily and said, "How did he know all that? I did not tell him anything." When the science was explained to her, she remarked, "It is all pretty true, I believe, only I do not think I am fond of 'ornament.' I have no rings, nor jewels, nor any such things, and I like my books a great deal more."

As early as thirteen, Sarah showed a natural ability to teach and gathered Africans around her, teaching them to read. Her behavior led Rev. Raymond to decide she was a born teacher and considered sending her to America for further education. When Mrs. Raymond became mentally ill, William realized he had no choice but to send her back to the United States and asked Sarah to go along as her traveling companion, with the understanding that Sarah would then be able to attend Oberlin College, which was the only college at the time to accept blacks.

While Raymond paved the way for Sarah to go to Oberlin, it was Lewis Tappan, by then secretary to the AMA, who supported Sarah financially. It was Raymond's hope that after Sarah completed her education she would head the girls' school he planned to establish at the Mission. Unfortunately, he died before his hope could be realized.

Writing to Lewis Tappan, Sarah told him of her studies: "I am studying very diligently so as to be qualified to do good in the world as this was my object in coming to Oberlin.... Don't forget me," she implored, "for I look to you as to a Father and if you forget me I don't know what I shall do." Indeed, she would have been unable to return to Africa without the financial assistance of Tappan.

"In 1845, while Sarah was at Oberlin, a terrible war broke out in the Sherbro country and continued several years. Many towns were burned and hundreds fled to the Mission for protection which, even amid these unfavorable circumstances, exerted a powerful influence for good."[31] The Mission school was sustained at great expense, for famine followed in the wake of war. Raymond was credited with rescuing a large number of children from bondage, thus saving them from slavery or death.

---

31   Rev. L. D. Bevan, DD, Africa, AMA Pamphlet No. 2, published by the AMA, NY 1878

Rev. Henry Badger, one of the English missionaries at Sierra Leone, wrote to a member of the AMA: "Did you ever hear of a mission being strengthened in the midst of war? Here is one, and it has advanced during the war more than previously."[32] The Mission, at first regarded with suspicion, was now looked upon with new respect. It was a sanctuary, and while other towns and places were being destroyed, the Mission continued to flourish and improve.

Rev. Raymond was a man of "rare capacity for work, and gained a wide influence among the people." He had a broad conception of the kind of mission needed in that country, and had, from the start, organized a manual labor school. The boys apprenticed to the carpenter's trade, as sawyers and as blacksmiths, and the girls assisted in cooking and taking care of the house and learned to sew. Raymond's plan was to make it a self-supporting mission, but, unfortunately, that was never realized.

Between 1841 and 1847, Raymond was the only member of the mission left, except for native assistants. In addition to his struggle to keep the Mission operating, he apparently lost the confidence of Lewis Tappan who was extremely critical of Raymond with respect to his perceived lack of business ability. However, it seems the major source of trouble was more personal. Tappan accused Raymond of showing improper attention to a female teacher at the Mission, but there was never any evidence to substantiate such an accusation. Indeed, after Raymond's death in November of 1847, he was portrayed by the AMA as the "great exemplar" for other missionaries to follow.

Eight months after the death of Raymond, the AMA recruited Reverends George Thompson and Anson J. Carter to serve at the Kaw Mendi Mission, despite heavy criticism leveled by Lewis Tappan relating to the circumstances of Thompson's recent release from prison. Thompson had served five years of a twelve-year prison sentence because of his efforts in aiding in the escape of slaves from Missouri. He had been subjected to torture, lack of food, cold, extremely hard labor, and even the possibility of being lynched during the ordeal. This, however, is not what bothered Tappan. An ardent abolitionist, Tappan wondered about the circumstances under which Thompson was pardoned from serving the full twelve years. Thompson had convinced the prison officials that he "repented of his crime, that he would never be guilty again, that he would discourage others from helping slaves to escape, and that he had lost his prejudices against slave-holders." He claimed that he had deliberately phrased his statements in such a way as to deceive his inquirers without stating a falsehood, but Tappan challenged

---

32    Ibid

that statement and wondered, "Can we trust a man whose intellectual & moral perceptions are so unsound?"

Tragedy struck just eight days after Thompson reached the Mission when Anson Carter died, leaving Thompson to carry on without any promise of help to follow. The American Missionary Association and others who followed Thompson's progress appeared not to appreciate his efforts. After many letters and pleas for missionaries, Thompson was surprised to learn that John S. and Fidelia C. Brooks and Sarah (Margru) Kinson had arrived in Freetown just two days after he had left.

Sarah had been corresponding with Thompson prior to leaving Oberlin and was warned in a letter from him: "If you have been tempted to get any fine dresses, or bonnets, give them away or throw them away, but do not bring them here." Thompson continued to worry about her fitness for missionary work but soon changed his mind when he found her trained to the nineteenth-century ideal of Christian womanhood—"pious, sexually pure, domestic, and submissive."[33]

Sarah was elated to be reunited with Maria (Te-me), the only other female from the *Amistad,* but she sorely missed her dearest friend, Charlotte (Kagne), who had died while Sarah was at Oberlin. She was also happy to see Lewis Johnson, Alexander Posey, and George Lewis, all of whom had become Christians and were valuable assistants to George Thompson.

Sarah lived up to Thompson's expectations as well as those of the AMA. The February 1851 issue of *The American Missionary,* a monthly publication of the American Missionary Association, reported:

> Sarah Margru Kinson seems to come fully up to the hopes of the Committee.... She is improving every day, and is doing all she can. Those who saw her when she was first arrived in this country, a captive in the Amistad and who labored for her release with that of the other captives, will rejoice at this, and bless God that he permitted them to snatch her out of the hands of a government that seemed eager to consign her, and her fellows to the tender mercies of an infuriated slaveholder.

On the other hand, after less than four years, Thompson's confidence in Lewis Johnson was no longer justified. In a letter to George Whipple dated February 24, 1854, Thompson wrote: "I have sad news to communicate. Kinna (Lewis Johnson), who shone so bright for a time has been, this evening in a church meeting, Excommunicated." Only three charges were filed:

---

33    George Thompson letter to Sarah dated May 24, 1849

1st Absenting himself for a long time from the Sacrament and all meetings.

2nd Breaking the Sabbath by going to Barmah on the Sabbath, for his business.

3rd Having two or more Wives!

**Kinna (Lewis) Johnson**

Taken from Barber's *History of the Amistad Captives* published in 1840

Johnson was present but said nothing. It was a solemn meeting according to Thompson, who explained to the membership how Johnson should be treated: "not to fellowship him, but yet count him not as an enemy, but admonish him as a brother."

Leaving the Mission in the hands of John Brooks and Sarah Kinson, Thompson, with the assistance of Thomas Bunyan, a native interpreter, made extensive expeditions into the Mendi country, where the many chiefs had been at war with each other for years. After two years, despite his frequent battles with acclimating fever which often left him prostrate, he managed to achieve success in his efforts to negotiate peace amongst the warring tribes.

Thompson fervently supported the abolition of the slave trade and was hopeful that the gospel missions in Africa would be a means of arresting this "abominable business." An article entitled "Mendi Mission" in the *Oberlin Evangelist* dated September 27, 1848, proclaimed: "Let the gospel elevate the pagans of Africa to Christian citizens, and they would cease to fight and enslave each other. The slave trade 'must die;' the Christian nations of the world would be stripped of their last apology for enslaving Africans."

Dedicated to the conversion of Africans to Christianity, Thompson worked toward that end, along with other missions in Africa, but his efforts were continually thwarted by the greed of both African and white slave traders. In addition, his continual pleas for more help seemed to fall on deaf ears and, after two years, his health had deteriorated to the point that he wrote to George Whipple: "John (Brooks) and myself have come to the conclusion that I should return home, as speedily as possible.... We feared if I should stay, I would certainly die, and then he would be left alone, after all." He added, "The fact that we are dying of overwork arouses no one."

Sarah was the only female teacher at the station when Thompson left. He was "much rejoiced," upon reaching New York, to find a company ready to start for Africa. He writes: "With great delight, I assisted to get them ready and on the 10th of December 1850 they sailed for the longed-for field."

Hannah More was among the company, a party of eight. J. C. Tefft and wife, F. L. Arnold and wife, Joanna Alden, William C. Brown, and Samuel Gray (colored) completed the group. According to Thompson, "They left in cheerful spirits, and arrived at their station safely."

Hannah and the other missionaries were transported from Freetown to the Kaw Mendi Mission in a small boat guided by Africans. After coming around a short bend in the river, Hannah saw a beautiful palm grove, consisting of a vast number of stately palm trees, their feather-shaped plumes bursting suddenly into view. Shortly thereafter, a two-story white Mission House, just eight rods from the river and about fifteen feet above the water, and a few other buildings could be seen.

FREETOWN. CAPITAL OF SIERRA LEONE.

**Freetown, Capital of Sierra Leone**
Taken from *The Palm Land*, by George Thompson.

As they came ashore, she was surprised at the number of buildings that comprised the Mission. There was a house of two rooms for boys; a rice and oil store; a goat house; and the chapel, standing a little back from the road, covered with bamboo thatch and walls made with mud. There was also a house for workmen; a large, new house for boys called the "Kaw Mendi Institute;" a carpenter's shop; and a cluster of variously shaped African houses.

Hannah was struck by the variety of beautiful flowers that had been planted by the missionaries and looked forward to planting the seeds that she had brought with her. Sometime later she wrote a poem which is partially quoted:

> This place to my heart is sacred and dear,
> Where our White House stood by the river clear;
> Majestic palm-trees wave their tufted plumes,
> And roses each month exhale their perfumes.
>
> Here stands the bread-tree, all loaded with fruit;
> And guavas, for jellies so much in repute;
> Plantains in clusters, so rich to behold,
> Bananas, in color like finest gold.

VIEW OF KAW MENDI MISSION.

**View of Kaw Mendi Mission**
Taken from *The Palm Land*, by George Thompson.

Here oranges grow, and lemons so fair,
Which white hands have planted and pruned with care;
The cashew-nut too, with its velvet-like flowers,
And then periwinkles which grace eastern bowers.

This garden's inclosed with a hedge of green,
Where sensitive plants and tulips are seen,
And marigolds raise their bright, golden heads,
While portulaccas bloom on their humble beds.

The arbor is graced with passion-flower vines,
And granadilla fruit in its shade reclines;
The sugar-cane too, yields its succulent sweet,
While rice and cassada, and fine yams they eat.

Hannah quickly adapted to the daily routine at the Kaw Mendi Mission, which was similar to that at the Dwight Mission. Rev. Thompson describes the daily activities of the Kaw Mendi Mission in his "Letters to Sabbath School Children."[34]

5:30 AM—A large bell would ring signaling that it was time to rise, wash and get ready for duty. In a few minutes the girls would go to the river to bathe.

6:00—The bell would ring again for the boys to wash and the workmen to commence work

6:30—The small bell would ring for the school to assemble for morning prayers

9:00—Mission family have breakfast

10:00–11:00—Intermission when the children and workmen have breakfast

11:00–2:00—School in session

2:00–4:00—Boys go to their respective work and girls go to sewing class

---

34    Thompson, George, *Letters to Sabbath-School Children on Africa,* Vols I through V, American Reform Tract and Book Society, Cincinnati, Ohio, 1858

After 4:00—Boys and girls are free to play, fish, swim etc. followed by dinner

**Evenings:**

Monday—Concert on first Monday of the month

Tuesday—Meetings in the chapel after which the ladies' class meets for instruction

Wednesday—General prayer-meeting

Thursday—Lecture in the chapel

Friday—Meetings held in chapel and in town

Saturday—Meeting in chapel and men's class after meeting

All missions under the AMA were organized as a family, i.e., the minister was looked upon as the father, and the missionary/teachers were thought of as mothers to the orphaned children. Each "family" usually consisted of twenty to thirty children. The "mothers" were responsible for ensuring that the children were kept clean and appropriately dressed and that they arrived on time for their meals and their classroom activities. The meals were prepared by a cook, who was assisted by the students and/or the missionaries when deemed necessary.

Children from nearby native families were also enrolled in the Mission school and commuted on a daily basis, but there was never enough income from tuition to support the Mission without assistance from churches in America. This support, by and large, came from New England and New York where Congregational churches were still in the majority.

After adjusting to the African climate and diseases of all kinds, Hannah was indefatigable in her efforts to seek support from churches in New York with which she had been associated before going to Africa, as well as her church in Union and the church in Willington where she had taught for several years. When boxes from these and other churches arrived, it was an occasion for celebration.

Thompson, along with his family and nine missionaries, returned to the Mission after two years of recuperation in the United States. His hopes for an increased staff to share the burden of running a Christian mission and school were greatly diminished by the loss of nearly half of those who had arrived in 1850. Hannah was the only woman in the group to survive. Miss Alden died three months after her arrival. Sister Tefft said, in her last moments, "Tell the friends in America, I die happy in the Lord, I can trust the Savior at this hour. I feel that I am going to Jesus's arms. I am not sorry that I came to Africa." Mrs. Arnold, according to Thompson's report, "felt thankful for the privilege of coming to Africa to labor for this degraded people, and often said, 'I have already been richly paid for coming to Africa.'"

On the other hand, one of the survivors, William C. Brown, turned out to be an agitator rather than a trusted helper. Initially they were impressed with him. "He is altogether different," wrote Rev. Franklin L. Arnold, "than we supposed he was, receiving his education as he did in one of the Southern States. Indeed, we consider him a noble young man, desiring to do the will of his blessed Master. He often says that he is willing to become a hewer of wood or a drawer of water if he may only be made wise in winning Souls to the Saviour and his actions fully confirm his words."

However, less than five months later, Arnold changed his mind when he learned of Brown's attempt to discredit Thompson by writing to the AMA on March 24, 1851, that Rev. Thompson was "definitely deranged in mind," that it would be wise to keep him quiet if possible, and pleading that he never again be placed in charge of the "temporal affairs of the Mission or he would certainly be mobbed."

Hannah More and J. C. Tefft joined with Arnold in condemning Brown as a "man lacking in integrity, a drunkard, and guilty of great extravagance." Brown left the Mission and joined the English missionaries, but they soon "found him out, and turned him off," and the last they heard of him, he was a tax collector in Sierra Leone.

There was a great concern among the missionaries about health issues. Thompson attempted to answer the often-asked question, why was the area "so sickly:"

> For let it be understood that all who go to Western Africa to reside, will, sooner or later, be called to pass through an acclimation, and will be more or less sick. Some will have a severe run of bilious fever, and many will die; while others will be more lightly affected, and after a few months enjoy good health. After the first fever, we are often troubled with "fever and ague," and general debility. We also suffer indescribably from ulcers, dreadful sores, boils etc.[35]

---

35  Thompson, George, *Palm Land of West Africa*, illustrated, Dawsons of Pall Mall, London, reprinted 1969

Having no idea, at the time, that mosquitoes carried malaria, they looked to other causes. Thompson wrote: "The cause of all this is found in the fact that vegetation is constantly growing and decaying, causing the rise of miasma, or poisonous vapor, which we are constantly inhaling or breathing. A thorough cultivation of the country would lessen, but never wholly remove this cause of sickness."[36]

Less than a year after her arrival, Hannah was given the entire supervision of all the girls at the Mission, in addition to overseeing all domestic matters. In a letter J. C. Tefft wrote to George Whipple, corresponding secretary of the AMA: "She is giving them daily lessons in domestic economy, sewing and other things for their real good. Her labors are arduous and responsible. Let her be especially remembered in prayer for, under God, the future destiny of this people is dependent upon her success."

Hannah's letter dated August 31, 1852, and addressed to the Eldridge sisters with whom she boarded in Willington, not only reflects her dedication to the cause of converting the "dark-minded" natives, but her feelings of isolation.

> Imagine how you would feel if you were hundreds of miles as I am from any other white woman. It is now near a year since I have seen a white female. I am such an anomaly here that as I raise mine eyes from my writing even now I behold people in the road gazing at me with mute astonishment! You may wonder at this till I tell you many of them have never seen a white woman and that I am not one among a thousand, but one among many thousands of colored ones in Africa at our station among the Mendians.
>
> Till recently (since this Mission has been established at the return of the Amistad Africans) heathen superstition, bigoted idolatry & intolerant Mohammedanism have swayed the minds of this people & no true light has dawned on them to dispel it. But since the establishment of this Mission our little Church numbers 30 & some half dozen are waiting for admission on the next Lord's Day.
>
> This little church seems truly to have "come forth from the wilderness leaning on her beloved & to look forth fair as the moon, clear as the sun and terrible to her enemies as an army with banners." Even now when war is devastating this country & dangers thicken on either side of us, the Mission seems a place of refuge.

---

36     Ibid

She went on to say how "pained" she was to see the naked women "exposed to the gaze of men with nothing to conceal their parts but a country cloth or girding of beads about their loins." The Mission lost no time establishing regulations intended to force members of the church and pupils of the school to wear clothing.

Neither was Hannah prepared for the myriad diseases which plagued the children at the Mission.

> Sometimes I bathe half a dozen sick children soon after I rise.... This morn I bathed five and dealt out twelve doses of medicine and administered most of it with my own hands. Shall I name some of the diseases which have prevailed here the past year and which it has not only been my lot merely to prescribe for, but to act both as physician and nurse? Measles, mumps, yaws, ringworm, congesting fever, pleurisy, prawcraws, dysentery, and leprosy, to say nothing of the more common ailments of children and youth or the infirmities of age. I can say that with God's blessing and my humble efforts, I have lost no patient.

When her scholars repented of their sins and accepted Jesus as their Savior, she felt that her efforts were amply rewarded. At such times, she said, "It has been my privilege to go among them, telling them in the most simple language of that blessed Savior who left all the glory of heaven and came down to earth to seek and save even the vilest of sinners and have entreated them to fling themselves unreservedly on his arms of mercy often kneeling and praying with and for them." She also rejoiced in the fact that many of her scholars "were in haste to get their education in order to go and tell their people about this Savior, to beg of them to renounce their idols, their country fashions and charms, their greegrees,[37] their devil bush, their fetishes, their witchcraft, mohamedism and polygamy."

> The other night I was awakened about midnight by the frightful screams of one of my older girls who asserted a witch had caught her by the neck and was strangling her. I tried hard to convince them from our

---

37   A Mohammedan Greegree could be a piece of paper, with a few Arabic letters and characters upon it, encased in leather or cloth, and usually suspended about the neck. A Pagan Greegree is a few leaves, or a little clay, or sand, or a pebble, or bark of a tree, incased in a cloth, or tied together. It is fastened to the wrists, ankles, and other parts of the body. They suppose these will keep off disease, and the intended injuries of enemies, preserve them from poisoned serpents, wild animals, keep off all evil, and secure all good. (Cite Fickenger's pg. 82)

lodging in the second story and the doors being locked, how impossible it was for anyone to enter the apartment. Besides there were no marks of violence on her neck, etc. But as that did not convince them, I commanded them to remain quiet till morning.

Then having assembled for worship, I expatiated on the folly of supposing a witch in a Mission House. I told them such a thing was unheard of in the annals of missions, remarking I had never seen a witch and never expected to see one. I represented it as so absurd they have not dared to broach it since."

Whether Hannah's rationale was sufficient to convince the girls, who had been born and raised in a society where witches were an integral part of their culture, that they were safe in a Mission House is questionable. She goes on to relate how a trial for one suspected of witchcraft was conducted:

The wizard is brought to the Palace or courthouse with the witnesses on both sides. If he is a married man with daughters, two of them are placed in his accuser's hands as hostages to be made slaves of in case he proves guilty.

The country pot is then placed over the fire with plenty of green sauce wood from the jungle which is deadly poison. They fill it with water and make it boil—during which they are to eat fricassee & palaver sauce. The liquor from the first is then presented him & he is told to drink plenty. If he is innocent it will cause him to vomit from the place where he sits even to the door, and disgorge his stomach not only of the poison, but of the fried chicken and palaver sauce, but if guilty he swells up & dies, a victim to folly and heathen superstition.

Sarah Kinson, a devout Christian, understood the fears of these young children and worked diligently to show them the way to Christ and salvation. She was also a determined young woman, and despite the objections of Hannah and others at the Mission, Sarah decided to marry Harry Tucker, an older student in the Mission boys' school and the son of a local African king who supported the slave trade yet sent his children to the Mission schools. Hannah and others felt Tucker would not support Sarah's commitment to the Mission since he had shown little interest in the missionary way of life, but their objections failed to change Sarah's mind. However, soon after her engagement, her fiancé was expelled from the Mission on charges of robbery. Their engagement was broken, and he moved away.

Just a year later, Sarah announced her engagement to Edward Henry Green, a new teacher in the boys' school. Educated in British mission schools in Freetown and converted to Christianity shortly before he came to Kaw Mendi, Green courted Sarah Kinson for six months. They were married in September 1852 with Hannah as a witness who complimented their wedding feast as "in good style." It was at this time that she heard the *Amistad* story from Sarah and four of the other captives: George Lewis (Ka-li), Maria (Te-me), Alexander Posey (Fa-ban-na), and Lewis Johnson (Kin-na) who were still at the Mission.

In reference to Sarah's new husband, Edward Green, she writes:

He was a grandson of a slave dealer. His father was born in Gambia on the Senegal River & was taken on board a Spanish Ship bound for Brazil, but was fortunately captured by an English Man-of-War. His mother was born on the Niger River, Upper Guinea & captured by a British Man-of-War. Thus they met and were united in the bonds of matrimony in the Colony of Sierra Leone where Edward, our hero, was born & educated. His conversion, he ascribes under God to a missionary sermon from the text, "Is thy heart right?" This led him to examine well the state of his heart and to know by happy experience the joy Religion can impart to cheer us in this wilderness world. Previous to this he had been a profligate young man. He frankly acknowledges it to be the transforming influence of the gospel that has made him what he is. The history of almost all at the time, if written out, would make an interesting volume. But it requires an abler pen than mine to do them justice.

After the wedding, Sarah and Hannah began an African women's sewing society, modeling it after similar ones in the United States. They named it the "Modest Dress Society." Its thirty-six members met weekly and were required to wear western-style clothes. Sarah, its first president, entertained the group with stories and informal sermons. But sometimes she felt discouraged. She wrote:

I am often tried, she said, tried with my school, tried with my neighbors; and tried with my missionaries, and am often tempted to leave the Mission. But when I call to mind, at such times, what the Lord has done for me in rescuing me from slavery, sparing my life to get an education, to cross the ocean four times, and to enjoy so many other favors at his hand, I feel that I cannot ever leave the mission work[38]

Edward Green, keeping pace with his wife's new role as a preacher, believed that the work of converting Africans should be done by the native-born like himself and Sarah. On New Year's Day, 1855, they left the station for the interior to start their own missionary station, but sometime later an accusation was made against Edward Green back at the Mission school. It was reported that during his time at the school he had seduced girls, sold them, and been intemperate. As a result of these accusations, he was dismissed from the Mission church.

Although Hannah had had high hopes for the success of this marriage, it was not to be. After Green's dismissal, Sarah's missionary career seems to have ended. There is no evidence of any correspondence from her after 1855 and no record of her death.

Continuing to labor at the Mission under trying circumstances, Hannah's courage was demonstrated when she and a male teacher, left alone at the Mission, found themselves confronted by about five hundred warriors. She wrote:

> They looked savage enough armed with cutlasses, knives, leopards teeth and greegree. Still I do not suppose there is a native woman in the region with half so much courage as I have. Unless our God takes care of us the Mission will surely be plundered. It seems to me the root of evil predominates in the hearts of this people to instigate them to any deeds of violence, oppression & cruelty they are capable of perpetrating. It looked sad to me, beyond expression, to behold the canoe load of slaves they have with them, whom they had just taken in the war with ropes about their necks & chains on their feet.

Hannah stood her ground, and the men went off, but two days later another war party stopped there and were at the point of beheading a man who had just purchased some rice from the Mission, when Brother Gray managed to stop them. Hannah wrote, "I think I do not fear death at all by the war, but I have feared to be taken captive by some of these base kings who have many wives. I should a thousand times prefer an innocent death.... A chill came over me as they landed, notwithstanding the thermometer stood at 88 degrees. The native women in the region flocked to me to let them into the house and yard for protection."

---

38    Lawson, Ellen MicKenzie with Marlene D. Merrill, *The Three Sarahs, Studies in Women and Religion*, Vol. 13, The Edwin Mellen Press, New York and Toronto, 1984

While Hannah was fearful of being taken captive by one of the African kings, there were hints of trouble regarding Thompson and the fate of the Kaw Mendi Mission. These stirrings were reflected in letters written to Thompson, who was then in America, by two missionaries and a son of an African chief. Brother Gray wrote:

> Almost every one wants to know when you are coming. They wish to see you very much ... there has been many discouraging things written against you, which at this time, there is none but what is sorry for it. I protested everything that came within my hearing but to no purpose. To say that you are not wanted here is a great mistake. If anyone is needed it is you.

George H. Decker wrote: "All the brethren are anxious to see you," and William Tucker, son of an African chief, who had been educated at the Kaw Mendi Mission wrote: "I am afraid if there is to be no Missionaries at all in this place what will be the state of our life?"

During the two years Thompson was in the United States he visited churches, made speeches about the necessity for financial support, and was unflagging in his efforts to recruit missionaries for Africa. He also managed to publish the book on which he had been working which was largely a description of the African people and Thompson's accomplishments in converting the natives to Christianity. It was promptly criticized by some as "misrepresentation and exaggeration."

After returning to the Kaw Mendi Mission with his wife and children, Thompson defended his work in a letter to George Whipple, secretary of the AMA.

> The charge of misrepresentation & exaggeration, I do most heartily repudiate. And say again, as I wrote to you once before that I have stated facts as they occurred in my experience & under my observation. If those same things do not always continue, if others come and do not see the things I did, but very different, am I, therefore, to be charged with misrepresentation? Yet this is exactly the case. And instead of quietly going forward & making things better some seem disposed rather to quarrel, because things are not as I spoke of! Make your future missionaries to understand they must expect trials, hardships and perhaps disappointments and come prepared to meet them & go on to save the people.

I suppose one reason why I get so many more kicks than others is because I write more & say more than the others & will not conform to their ways which I disapprove. But I will try to bear patiently the buffeting both for my faults & for my well doing.

Hannah More, Dr. Flickinger, Jane A. Winters, Mr. and Mrs. Tefft, and Susan Woolsey signed a statement addressed to the American Missionary Association in defense of Thompson:

> Bro. George Thompson, who has labored long and hard and alone, bearing the heat and burden of the day, when there was no other to labor in this sickly field—has been charged by some with exaggeration and misrepresenting the success of the Gospel here & the ripeness of the African field. We desire, hereby, to say without hesitation & with emphatic earnestness, that so far as we have yet seen, and had experience in the same field, we feel that he has *not* used any exaggerated statements, or given too glowing colors, respecting either the past success of the Gospel here, the present condition of the people & children, or the future prospects of this wide and ripe field, if the men and means could only be had to 'Go up & possess the Land' as the Lord requires & as the indications of His Providence urge us speedily to do. What we ourselves have seen is even beyond any glowing statement we ever saw from Bro. Thompson or any other one. To enter heartily into the work of doing the people good & saving their souls, is to see, and experience such like seems as Bro. T. has described.

Thompson's trials were not limited to the problems of overseeing the Mission. Tragedy struck just a few months after his return from the United States when his son, George, became ill. Despite Hannah's and Martha Thompson's devoted ministrations, little George died at the age of five and one-half years. At the funeral, Hannah "spoke movingly, in an excellent and deep feeling prayer," according to Thompson.

George and his wife were devastated by the death of their first-born child. He wrote: "Who would have thought that the sprightly, ever active, laughing George, would be the first of our company to fall! We thought it not." Their remaining son, Moses, also became very sick, requiring constant attention. A few days later Hannah and Miss Sexton were also taken sick. Hannah and the Thompsons, along with Moses, found it necessary to travel to Freetown in hopes that a different atmosphere would be beneficial.

After a few weeks there, Dr. Deane, a resident physician in Freetown, determined that Moses's only hope was to leave Africa and return to the United States.

Martha, constantly worried about Moses, was very ill as well. Thompson decided that it would be best for him to return with his family.

It fell to Hannah to take on Thompson's work as well as her own. In addition to managing the Mission school, caring for the gardens, nursing the children through a mumps epidemic, and tending to the new missionaries who were undergoing acclimating fever, Hannah also began to preach on Sundays when George Thompson was away.

She described her feelings in a letter dated February 16, 1856: "I was educated in the strictly puritanical sentiment of New England and early became a member of a Congregational church where women speaking in meetings was reprobated as highly censurable." She continued in the same letter:

> One night in particular I recollect with what vividness a sermon came to my mind so strong as in imagination I preached it that I could recollect it in the morning. Still I tried to suppress the monster within & dared not mention to my most intimate friends the struggle which was going on within. After long resisting the influences of the Spirit till the burden became almost intolerable I arose in an evening Meeting & gave vent to my feelings in an exhortation.

> I cannot portray on paper this change which passed in my mind. Instantaneously the burden was removed & the choking, agitated feelings gone, the palpitating heart beat more uniform & the tremulous voice became clear & distinct. Some Baptists remarked with wonder, that I had not used my talents before & I was afterward informed by their minister 'they could have staid all night to have heard such speaking.'

> Still my own church people & family were as opposed as ever to females speaking in public. Scarce ever did I have an opportunity among them, but if any occurred which I neglected to improve, my burdened spirit could not be releaved (sic) till I had confessed my guilt to God and promised amendment.

While she was pleased to be given the opportunity to preach and enjoyed teaching the African children, she was increasingly aware of problems within the Mission and came to the conclusion that it would be best to move to another location. In light of the extraordinary events that would occur two years later, the following letter written by Hannah to George Whipple in March of 1854 leads one to wonder why Hannah was so distraught when the Mission was, in fact, torn down.

Reasons for removing the station:

1st—The location is unhealthy

2nd—The school is too large numbering 100 pupils

3rd—They all eat in the yard—the boys' tables under the wings of the house next to the basement and the girls' house close by

4th—Missionaries and children lodging in the house usually between 30 & 40 leaving the inner rooms not well ventilated causing us to inhale too much carbon and too little oxygen. This might be tolerated in New England but ought not to be in a low mangrove swamp like those near us.

5th—We have too many of the Tucker children here. The parents of some of them have paid board and tuition and clothed them in the Colony, a number of the children are now dependent for all on the Mendi Mission.

6th—Bad water at this season of the year, unless we send ¾ of a mile for it.

Stating that she thought her experience was "worth something," she added:

Our house is too central—there are too many people around us. The chapel is so near we can hear the preaching and stay home. This renders it very unpleasant for me when I teach. It is for this reason that I do not wish the lectures I give the children (made) public, and I do not wish to disturb sick people with noise either in school or out.

To illustrate her point she cited the success of the Seminaries in the Choctaw Nation in which classes were held in a building one-quarter mile from the Missionary Station. "The schools were considered under the best management that were located at least out of hearing of any other house."

Thompson, in the meantime, wrote letters to the AMA reporting the errors and shortcomings of his fellow laborers, including Hannah. The Mission became hopelessly divided into discordant factions with little promise of improvement. Attacks and counterattacks regarding Thompson continued. He was excoriated by John Brooks, a long-time associate and supporter, as a "madman." Brooks cited a situation he had observed where Thompson baptized people who, according to Brooks, had no interest in the proceedings whatever and later, during the communion service, the bread was not consecrated, and some children who were not "professors of religion" were allowed to take both the cup and bread. Brooks stated that it was "most likely through carelessness or lack of regard for the solemnities of the occasion," but he was grieved by the carelessness manifested and thought the ordinances of the Church must suffer if such things were allowed to be repeated.

Whether Thompson was aware of these reports is not known. He seemed more relaxed after his return from America and recounts a Christmas expedition in 1854 when they all went to Barmah:

> After breakfast, we prepared our canoes and boats, filled them with merry, happy children, overseen by the teacher, Miss More, and myself and rode to Barmah in high glee and joyous spirits—all feeling the need and benefit of a few hours recreation. Two and two we all marched into the barricaded town, and ranged ourselves about the king's yard, he sitting in his hammock beneath his piazza, while his numerous wives and the people of the town crowded around to see a sight the most of them never saw before—a large company of well dressed, orderly, intelligent and smiling children, rendered thus through the elevating influences of Christianity.
>
> For an hour we sang many of our best pieces, on which the school had been previously drilled. It was an interesting scene, and the poor ignorant country people seemed to enjoy it very much. After we were through, the children were to run about awhile and see the town. Kalifah, to do us honor, sent a man to off his large cannon. We believe that the effect of our visit was salutary.

Hannah's impressions of this expedition are interesting and provide a more detailed accounting, including her speech against slavery and the plight of African women, and later her embarrassment when "exposed as a show to the ignorant and rabble."

> Our scholars spoke to large audiences in Catamahoo and Harnhoo, walled or barricaded cities, where the Palaver Houses were open to us on the occasion. Our scholars acquitted themselves nobly on the occasion, speaking in Eng., Sherbro and Mendi on polygamy and its evils in form of dialogue, etc.
>
> I spoke against slavery, war etc. through an interpreter and with a view to raise women from the degradation to which she is doomed among this barbarous people. I was gazed at with wonder and astonishment being the first white woman ever seen by many of them.

Br. Thompson and our interpreter also spoke on the importance of civilization, beautifully contrasting the superiority of the Kaw Mendi school with the barbarity of the naked ones around us.

Our scholars did credit to themselves and, as I trust, awakened a desire for education among the natives they could have done in no other way. So we, our boats and canoes with flags and banners hoisted, made a display on the Rivers and the childish glee of the children seemed so different from their war canoes that I wonder not that it should speak volumes on the utility of education.

As they continued their journey down river, they were hailed from shore on order from the King that they must come to the landing so that the people might behold a white woman. "I felt rather indignant," she wrote, "and tried to persuade our captain not to stop, but as I was the only white person in the boat my entreaties were useless and I was exposed as a show to the ignorant and rabble."

After returning to Kaw Mendi, she expressed her belief that nothing would be done to remove the station, especially since she did not believe it was God's will. "God will doubtless overrule for good to this people and to us whose labors have been so abundant for their benefit."

In the meantime, the American Missionary Association, all too aware of the chaotic situation at Kaw Mendi, began interviewing potential candidates to take charge of the Mission. In view of the excessive number of deaths at the Kaw Mendi Mission, they were looking for a medical doctor with strong ties to a church, who might eventually become ordained. Dr. David Lee had written the AMA regarding missionary work in China and was told that the Association had no missions in China, but there was a pressing need for missionaries in Africa. In a correspondence with the AMA, Lee said he had been reading *Thompson in Africa*, which had given him much "light upon the subject" and that Mrs. Lee was also delighted with the prospect of "usefulness that is opened up before her in such a land as that, and is ready to sacrifice the comforts of her native land and willing to consecrate herself to the missionary cause."

He went on to say: We do not belong to the Allopathic School. Our views and principles are very different from those advanced upon disease in general, and more particularly in reference to the acclimating process which emigrants to that country pass through. In that respect we agree with Bro. Thompson that no strong medicines i.e. no poisons, should be used, indeed we discard them altogether. Our system is founded upon physiological laws and our remedies always of a sanitary character. Our success in practice, leads us to believe we would be instrumental in saving many of the lives of valuable missionaries should we be sent to Africa. This too is one of the motives that prompt us to offer ourselves to your board. We, with Br. Thompson, discard the use of coffee, wine and all alcoholic stimulants whatever in beverages. We are now partially acquainted with Phonotophy and Phonography[39] and intend to devote more attention to it before we would sail that we might be useful as translators whatever station we might be called upon to fill. We hope to be able to discharge its duties however arduous and pressing.

The Mission Board was careful to seek references regarding Dr. Lee and his wife, Martha, who was also a medical doctor. They conducted probing interviews realizing that the situation at Kaw Mendi would require a strong leader with good communication and organizational skills.

The AMA accepted the Lees, and they arrived at Kaw Mendi December 5, 1855. Thompson described their reception:

The whole school at once formed in double lines in front of the chapel—so that the newcomers could walk between them, and sang one of their favorite pieces while the strangers passed along. It was an affecting and interesting moment. They were always glad to greet new missionaries, but more especially now, since so many had died and the laborers were few.

Dr. Lee was unexpectedly impressed with the Mission school saying:

The half has not been told of the bright side here. Few schools in the United States will compare with this one, in their declamation, composition, etc. considering all things. I am astonished at the rapidity with which these children learn. They acquire a knowledge of their studies much faster than children in America.

Hannah couldn't have agreed more. She had often written about the prowess of her students, saying, "The children of this school have made more rapid progress than those of any other school I have taught."

---

39   Phonotophy and Phonography are ways of phonetically translating a language

Dr. Lee went on to say:

> I found the school here in great need of a good teacher. Miss Moore is almost chrushed (sic) with the care of 80 children and we have no native teachers. We expect one by the 1st of Jan. I am arranging the school and find many bright geniuses among them. Some of the brethren have no doubt informed you of our intention to remove this station to Wela. We must do it or all die off and if it is not done Mrs. Lee and I will go to some other station. Can you not send us help, we want someone to assist us, not be in our way, nor want us to wait on them? We all work hard here and I beseech you to send no Allopathic Physicians here. We are so well united now it would be a pity to spoil the harmony.

> My past sickness and deep suffering have endeared me to my work. I feel more like living for God than I have ever done. My vivacity and buoyancy, I think, will return and I will still love this climate. I more than ever feel like staying in Africa.

Dr. Lee's treatment of intermittent fever differed from that of George Thompson, but they did agree that quinine or calomel, alcoholic liquors (as medicine), and other strong drug remedies were not effective in Africa. Thompson was a firm believer in the hydropathic method of treatment which involved cold water baths and drinking quantities of warm water: "I am still, as for years, firm in the conviction, that no system of therapeutics is so well adapted to cure the diseases of Africa as the pure system of hydropathy, when properly and faithfully applied by skillful hands."

Hannah, on the other hand, believed in the Allopathic treatment which consisted of fomentations, or hot and cold compresses alternately applied, along with sudorific drinks which induced perspiration. The hot poultices consisted of a soft, heated mass of meal or clay. This was only the first of many fundamental disagreements that would alienate her from the Lees.

Prior to a meeting of all members of the Mission to discuss the proposed removal of the Kaw Mendi Station, Hannah and Dr. Lee exchanged views, but it wasn't long before Hannah was convinced that "her views were considered not worth listening to." Summarizing the discussion in a letter to Lewis Tappan, she wrote of her conviction, based on past experience, that any new location would be unhealthy for a number of years until the soil was turned up, cultivated, and kept clean. Why abandon Kaw Mendi when it had already gone through the process! To do so "looks to me ominous of evil."

All that was necessary, in Hannah's opinion, was to "keep everything neat about the dwellings and when necessary use chloride of lime and ammonia where malaria prevails." When she said she thought her fifteen years on mission ground had not been in vain, Lee responded "a little common sense was worth lots of such experience, and that my (Hannah's) experience was not based on logical premises and was good for nothing." "So much for common sense," Hannah wrote. The discussion ended when he said, "You are not going to oppose us in our new measures are you?" She replied, "I will oppose you in whatever measures I deem wrong or impracticable."

When the Lees convened the meeting of the Mission members, Hannah was just getting ready for her next class and decided it was her duty to stay with the children, especially since there was no one with whom she could leave them. "It seemed to me duty called me to the School and having confidence in my brethren's unanimous opinions, I imprudently said 'I will not oppose you in whatever measures you all unite in.'" After the meeting, "the first salutation from the Mission House was, 'we have voted to remove Kaw Mendi and are waiting for your signature.'" "I was greatly surprised, but said nothing till I found opportunity to speak with Br. Thompson alone. When I told him I did not think he would accede to the measure, and inquired what I must do— had I gone to God I should have done better, but I had given my word not to oppose them."

The thought of a healthier location and the fact that it might take at least three or four years before a place could be found and buildings erected sufficient to accommodate so large a school led Hannah to think that nothing was going to happen very soon. In fact, she said she "might be in the grave," before the changes took place.

Later, she had second thoughts about having signed the article in 1856 to remove Kaw Mendi and wrote to Rev. Whipple: "I feel that I did wrong in so doing and on my knees have begged pardon of God.... My heart was never in it and my motive for doing it was peace, remembering your admonition that the minority should ever yield to the majority which would seem to be right among Christians any and everywhere."

The Mission members, following the recommendation of Dr. and Mrs. Lee, voted to remove the Kaw Mendi Mission because of its unhealthy location next to a swamp and because of the contaminated water supply. It was obvious to the Lees that the reason for so many deaths at this Mission, compared to the lower death rate at other Missions in the area, was the location. Indeed, two years earlier, Hannah had recommended that the Kaw Mendi Mission be moved, but no action had been taken. Now Dr. and Mrs. Lee, newcomers to the area, had the temerity, in Hannah's opinion, to make a similar recommendation which was accepted. Whether either Hannah or Rev. Thompson was aware that there was a second recommendation to come out of the meeting—that Thompson and More be replaced—is not known. In any event, Hannah wasted no time in making her opposition known to the AMA regarding the proposed removal of Kaw Mendi, while Thompson seemed to accept the recommendation. Thus ended the unity and harmony reported earlier by Dr. Lee.

The American Missionary Association was not quick to respond to Hannah's letters in which she said she preferred to "labor among the natives rather than the missionaries." She wrote:

> I would, by all means, prefer being located at a station with native help-
> ers or not more than one missionary. And I still give it as my opin-
> ion, founded on experience, that Missionaries should ever be scattered
> among the natives, leaving merely enough to direct at the station where
> native helpers are to be obtained and who are qualified for the work.

Her recommendations stemmed, without a doubt, from her experience at the Dwight Mission, where, according to Hannah, there were too many missionaries and not enough qualified native workers, or in other words, "too many chiefs and not enough Indians."

Hannah's deep emotional stress showed in the following letter written to Brother Tappan on February 26, 1856, after learning that the Kaw Mendi Mission had been destroyed. She was "recruiting her health" in Freetown, and Thompson was traveling in Liberia when she wrote:

> It is with painful emotions not to be described, I seat myself to address
> you. My heart is full of sorrow. Again I am a homeless stranger in a
> strange land. Two days have elapsed since I heard of the downfall of
> Kaw Mendi. Had it been by relentless War by the hands of ruthless
> Savages that it had been broken down, ransacked and burned, then I
> could have held my peace and borne it.
>
> But I will lay my hand on my mouth in mute astonishment while
> I announce to you it was done by those with whom I have taken sweet
> counsel and walked to the house of God in Company. Yes, Dr. Lee, I
> learn has done the infamous deed with the advice and consent of the
> brethren and sisters of God and Kaw Mendi in the absence of both Br.
> Thompson and myself and without our being consulted in the impor-
> tant matter of pulling down the Kaw Mendi Mission House.
>
> Is not the language of the prophet appropriate on this occasion?
> "Hear O Heavens and give ear O Earth for the Lord hath spoken and I

have nourished and brought up children, but they have rebelled against me!"

I am informed the natives took up arms to defend it, but were repulsed by Dr. Lee who would not have hesitated to have used his revolving pistol had he deemed it necessary. They were then bringing the Mission House and its effects to Good Hope there to be put up at auction and sold to the highest bidder! Is it just, thus to meddle with Br. Thompson's or my private property in our absence? You may recollect I paid you for my bureau and brought money of my own earnings with me for other furniture. My silver spoons and dishes for the table have been in common use. But when you call to mind that I am a year older than Mrs. Tappan and am left houseless, homeless and penniless among strangers your sympathies will, I trust, be awakened.

My own Dear Mother who consecrated me to the Lord, even from the womb, lies low in the grave, peace to her memory, having died since I have been laboring as a Missionary in Africa. My Father's handsome estate, I learn, is mostly disposed of, he having secured the house and home farm to my brother for his support. As I did not marry to please him, but enlisted in the Mission Cause it is very little I can claim or expect from that source.

Intelligence from the American Missionary Association has reached me that I am not needed there. Indeed, I heard it discussed myself before leaving Kaw Mendi that a man and his wife and a single lady were enough to occupy a single Station. If my God tells me it is my duty to go and live in a country house and among the Natives, I think I should not hesitate to go. Still I am aware I am not destitute of that shrinking female delicacy so much admired in our sex.

Little did I think when I gave the parting hand to my Associates and loved pupils, who gathered around me with so much warmth of feeling, some of them weeping aloud, as they grasped my hand and I gave them my maternal benediction, requesting them to be good children until my return, that the costly edifice where we had spent so many happy hours, would, ere my return, be laid in ruins and those loved ones sent back to heathenism. Somehow I felt Sad as I heard them repeat "Miss More, you love us, but these other ones, Aha, Oyer!! Oyer!" Interrupted by sobs. As I entered the canoe and proceeded to Good Hope my sadness was uninterrupted although Miss McIntosh tried her best to console me, telling me as I was going to recruit, cares should be banished and my mind be at rest.

Though it has cost much labor amid many discouragements to bring the Kaw Mendi pupils out of the mental darkness in which I found them shrouded, I feel that my efforts have not been in vain in the Lord. Many would doubtless have been disheartened by the arduous work of drawing out the minds of these ignorant natives and teaching them to think and act for themselves.

I can say, in truth, that even in boasted America, where I have taught many years, never have my white or Indian pupils surpassed these native sons of Africa in either mental arithmetic, grammar, and I might add, astronomy, philosophy and natural history, botany, physiology and in writing compositions and declaiming I have not had their equals in America.

Thus you see Kaw Mendi has never been in so flourishing a condition as during the past year. It has not only mentally and spiritually, but literally budded and blossomed as the rose. Indeed, I do not think a single week has elapsed, and I am in doubt whether a day, that our beautiful rose bushes have not been in bloom. We never have been able, till the last year, to have a flower garden.

Those seeds sent me by our friend, Sarah Hamhurst, have made our garden at Kaw Mendi the beauty and wonder of all that section of country. It occupies the same ground on which a battalion of reckless savages once stood, firing their artillery and flourishing their swords, spears and cutlasses in front of the Mission house when the school children were clinging, affrighted, to my clothes. The same plot of ground was in beauty blooming with American flowers when I left. I shall ever remember that eventful period of my Missionary life.

On the same date Hannah wrote a letter addressed to Dr. Lee and the M. M. Missionaries which precipitated an immediate and unprecedented action. The letter is quoted in full:

Surely the Lord will plentifully reward the proud doers for judgements (sic) are prepared for Scorners and Stripes for the backs of Fools as says Solomon's Prov.

Can it be considered one whit better than sacrilege, thus impiously to reach forth an arm of flesh, against a Mission House razing it even to the foundations thereof? Do we not behold with detestation the ruthless mob who would ransack, pillage, & destroy property? How much more nefarious must it seem in the sight of Him who looketh on the Heart when such as bear the name Missionaries set up at Public Auction, Mission and individual property earned and contributed by labors with prayers, tears, and strong crying to the Mission? thus desecrating it from a sacred to a common use!

Forbid it Almighty God!

Are not Common Sense and Worldly wisdom synonymous terms? Would not either of them, for their own Emolument, deprive those worthier than themselves of house and home, leaving them to the tender mercies of the Wicked which are indeed cruel.

> My weapons are not carnal but
> Mighty through God to the pulling
> Down the strongholds of Satan: Paul

I had rather venture myself among natives than with such as bear the Christian name unless their Religion would keep them [from] invading the rights of others. How many of you should have the cupidity to meddle with Br. Thompson's or my personal property in our absence is a question I am not prepared to solve? I am ignorant of Data empowering you to do so, having never seen credentials authorizing you to remove the Kaw Mendi Station.

Have we not been imposed on too much to trust to the verbose sayings of strangers? I leave all in the hands of (a) just and holy Being assured he will give us all right ~ ~~ Knowing there is no Wisdom, nor counsel, nor understanding against the Lord and that he will never lay on any one more than right. In him I cast my burden well knowing he will sustain me.

*Hannah More*

**Good Hope Mission Station (site of the unprecedented meeting). The Mission House is on the right and the Chapel on the left.**
Taken from a drawing by Rev. J. S. Brooks and later published in an American Missionary Association publication, August 1856.

Fifteen days later, Hannah received an answer, called the "Address," from her associates: David and Martha Lee, D. W. Burton, and Mrs. L. A. Tefft, with a codicil from George Thompson saying that although he could not be present at the meeting, he fully agreed with the proceedings. A separate statement from John S. Brooks, who was then at Boom Falls Station, also agreed with the "Address."

Good Hope Mission Station
March 12, 1856

Dear Sister:

At a meeting of your associates and fellow laborers in this mission, held the above date—Your letter of Feb. 25th, 56 was taken under consideration, and after mature deliberation thereon, in connection with past and present circumstances connected with this mission, it has been deemed necessary to the peace and unity of action among us, to send you the following address, a copy of which has been sent to the Executive Committee of the American Association, and a copy retained with us. Your letters have also been forwarded to the same authorities and a copy of a note sent with them, is herewith included.

Address ~~~~

Whereas—There has been from time to time many letters written pro and con between the members of this mission, that have been a source of ill feeling and unchristian conduct toward each other; and whereas these communications are always uncalled for and disgraceful to the parties concerned in them. But more particularly did we consider your letter of 25th Feb. 1856, as being unmerited on your part, and on your part exceedingly abusive, insulting, and unchristian in its tone—impugning our moral characters as honest, peace loving men and women. We consider you altogether unjustified in writing it. For the reasons that you well understood and acquiesced in the removal of Kaw Mendi and signed resolutions to that purpose some months since, also that had you considered your brethren so dishonest as not to be trusted with either mission or private property, you should have before this, reported them to the proper authorities.

We therefore deem it our Christian duty to you, as one of our co-laborers, to faithfully show you your wrong in penning that or any more such letters to your associates, and ask you to retract your accusations against us. Should you do so, you will add a still stronger tie to our united action in these labors of love, if you will give us your promise that you will cooperate in our actions when unanimous, as was the removal of Kaw Mendi Station and when consistent with the Glory of God and the good of the perishing heathen for whom we labor.

Should you, however, persist in maintaining the sentiment contained in the letter concerning your fellow laborers, we cannot consistently ask you to continue your connection with us, well knowing that the characters therein ascribed to us, could not give to you the Christian fellowship so much to be desired in a mission field, and however painful it may be to us, we must acquiesce in your withdrawal from us and return to the United States or to such field of labor as shall be agreeable to you.

We deem this action in your case necessary to forever remove, if possible, the cause of any more of those disagreeable and disgraceful bickering, which have too often wrung our hearts and been a source of reproach from our enemies.

This action in the matter is final, and we expect your reply at the earliest opportunity, as we desire to arrange our plans for the future.

We remain Yours for every good word and work.

Signed:    David J. Lee
           D. W. Burton
           L. A. Tefft
           Martha C. Lee

Though not present at the above meeting, I can say I fully agree therewith Signed: George Thompson

As I have written to sister More on the subject of her note, I could wish to see her reply before signing this, but believing the above, not only just, but really called for, I cannot decline cooperating with my associates in the above address.

Boom Falls Station M.M Mo Tappan House—15th March 1856
Signed: John S. Brooks

Dr. Lee issued an ultimatum to the AMA:

If, however, the committee disapprove of our operation and condemn our course in reference to Kaw Mendi and Miss More and they see proper to return Mr. Thompson and Miss More to the Mission, we have no other alternative than to consider ourselves recalled and must leave the work. We have acted from principle and cannot go back. We came unprejudiced in favor of any party in the Mission and if we pleased or displeased the others, self was not the motive.

It would be at least a month before an answer could be expected from the American Missionary Association. Hannah's future was at stake. The newly arrived Lees had made it clear that if Thompson and More were allowed to stay then they had no other recourse but to leave.

Having recovered his health, Thompson went on an extensive tour in Liberia and was not heard from for several weeks. Rumors were rife which raised concerns at Kaw Mendi. In a letter dated March 1856, Hannah wrote to George Whipple:

The sad intelligence has reached us that the Boat in which Br. Thompson went to Liberia is lost & they have already raised a loud cry at Kaw Mendi & I cannot think the weeping or wailing has been feigned. The report is that some of them are lost overboard & that a Man-of-War ship picked up some of them. We have some faint hope that Br. Thompson may be safe & for this I will continue to pray till the cloud of doubt disperse & facts are brought to light.

Thompson recorded in his book, *Thompson's West Africa*, that he had "some very narrow escapes among the breakers at Sea Bar" but was not prepared for the greeting he received on March 13, 1856, when he arrived at Good Hope and was met by Dr. Lee, who said, "I never expected to see you again." Later, when he arrived at Kaw Mendi, he was astonished by the reception he received:

> When we came around a point in the river, which brought us in sight of the village near Kaw Mendi, where some of the relatives lived, the whole people instantly were greatly excited. They clapped their hands and shouted, threw up their arms jumped in wild excitement, and ran to the Mission to meet us.
>
> Old and young also crowded to embrace me, and shake my hand, and some of the old mothers threw their arms around, and would not cease thanking me, for bringing back their sons again, and coming myself, as they never expected to see their old minister again. It was a very affecting scene, which I can never forget.

A meeting was held in April 1856 that was intended to identify and correct some critical issues at all the Missions. George Thompson and Tefft sent letters excusing themselves on account of sickness. Hannah was not among the attendees, and there was no indication as to whether she had been invited.

The new rules and regulations were meant to guide the newer Missions, but they also recognized that improvements were needed at the oldest Mission, and, therefore, voted to "appoint a committee of missionaries, on the ground, to examine the condition of Kaw Mendi and report the same with a plan for its improvement believing that by some changes which might easily be made, it would become not only an ornament to our Mission, but one of the best schools on the West Coast of Africa and at the same time lessen considerably its expense."

The report went on to explain away some of the problems which the people of the Missions were experiencing by saying: "By the experience of the past we are admonished of the increased danger to which we are exposed by the unhappy effect of the climate on the temper, of receiving and harboring unpleasant personal feelings toward each other, tending greatly to disturb the peace and prosperity of our Mission."

Thompson, they reported, "objected to all and declared his intention to at once abandon the Mission on account of them. It is hoped that his objections lay in a misunderstanding of them and that after they shall be kindly and fully explained, he will look upon them with more lenity."

Thompson, himself, wrote:

> It was thought best, on the whole, to have no more white missionaries locate at K.M., but carry on the operations there through a native

agency. If the large house remained, it was thought that new missionaries would desire to go to a place of which they had heard so much, and would there prematurely sicken and die, as so many others before them had done; therefore the house itself should be removed, leaving sufficient buildings for any native laborers needful to carry on the work.

On the surface, Thompson agreed about the necessity for reducing the size of the Kaw Mendi Mission, but it was a painful decision after having put so much of himself into the success of the Mission. He did not know, at the time, that Dr. Lee had not been given authority by the Mission Association to tear the main buildings down. He described his feelings in a letter to Louis Tappan:

> I write to say that a new dynasty has arisen with authority and having the disposition to pull down what I have labored and suffered for so earnestly for seven years and I feel that I cannot bear to see it.
>
> Let me be away that my ears be not tortured by the groans of distress. When I came out first you instructed us to be very careful in introducing any new changes, contrary to those the people had from Raymond, lest they should become prejudiced against us. It was prudent advice. But Dr. Lee comes instructed to remove this station! A most wild preposterous idea.... I wish not to stand in the way.

Lee and Thompson were destined to have a falling out. The following incident, described by Dr. Lee in a letter to George Whipple dated March 9, 1856, was the last straw:

Both Dr. Lee and his wife, Martha, were ill and in bed when "to add to our misery, Thompson turned his great baboon loose in the rooms—he screamed and made all kinds of noise." Moments later the "baboon came bounding and screaming into our room, stealing articles from our table and finally ending up under our bed." As Dr. Lee arose from his bed in an effort to oust the baboon, he "turned around and beheld Thompson watching the whole affair and doing nothing. In an unguarded moment, I called to him to take out his baboon, that he was more like one than anything else. Now I was sorry at once that I had said it, and confessed my wrong and am really sorry for it."

A similar story was circulated among the missions in Freetown which, in turn, stimulated Capt. and Mrs. Sumner, who were English missionaries, to write to the AMA in defense of Thompson.

> As so many scandalous reports are in circulation we feel called on to state some facts that have passed under our roofs and before our eyes....

Mr. Thompson has been two months with us and we can testify to his uncommonly peaceful and mild deportment. We would not put up with such treatment as he has received from Dr. and Mrs. Lee, and hold our peace, but we do not think that many in Freetown would. He has, in our presence, been called a liar, an adulterer and worse than a murderer and beneath a baboon.

Astonished when Thompson did not defend himself, they told the Lees as well as Mr. and Mrs. Burton, who were also missionaries, to seek lodging elsewhere. They concluded: "We tell you these things hoping you will put a stop to this at once by recalling Dr. and Mrs. Lee forever, keeping out of your mission field such abominable characters and such villains in human shape."

The Lees were not recalled, and the situation continued to deteriorate. Unable to contain her anger concerning the destruction of the Kaw Mendi Mission, Hannah wrote letter upon letter to George Whipple. Delivery of letters, it should be pointed out, was dependent solely upon ships which took at least a month and, more often, forty days one way, so that any decisions made by the Association could not be expected for at least two months.

Hannah's several letters over a period of two months were answered, but not the way she might have hoped. Rev. Whipple reported that her letters caused a great deal of distress. "In the case of our departed brethren and sisters, our loss and Africa's loss is their gain, but where is the gain, when we lose, the mission loses, and Africa loses, and God is dishonored by the strife and contention of his professed children!" He went on to say:

At this distance it is difficult for us to say who the troubler is, or to decide whom we may recall with hope of this, at once, removing the cause of the dissensions and heart-burning that exists there. I doubt whether calling home of any one will do this. Feeling thus, I turn to the more grateful, tho still painful task, of endeavoring to secure harmonious cooperation among you all. How honorable to you all, and how acceptable to the blessed savior it would be, if this could be accomplished. I am sure it can be done, if each one would consider self as nothing; and the cause of missions, the honor of God, as all. Will you not thus feel and act leaving yourself, your feelings, your reputation, etc., to be vindicated by God, while you give yourself wholly to the work of converting the heathen and training them to a life of holiness?

Regarding the removal of the Kaw Mendi station, Whipple confirmed Hannah's suspicion that Dr. Lee was not given authority to dismantle it, but waffled by saying that Dr. Lee may have thought he had that approval and that maybe it was a wise move after all. Whipple continued:

> I do not find any record of the Committee, or any line of instruction given to Dr. Lee or remember of having any conversation with him, nor of hearing others converse with him, which could be construed as authority given to him to remove the K. M. station. And yet I do not doubt that, if he has said he had such authority, he honestly thought he had. Probably he must have supposed that he derived it from something that some one of the officers or members of the committee may have dropped in conversation. If the Com. had meant to give any such authority they would have put it on record. No such authority was given; yet I conceive it very possible that Dr. Lee supposed he had authority. While I fear that evil may result from reducing the station so hastily, and feel a regret that the Ex. Com. were not consulted about it before hand, I am not certain that its speedy reduction may not prove to have been wise.
>
> At any rate, the thing is done and however much the doing of it may have rent our hearts and alarmed our fears, our duty now is to do the most good we can in the circumstances. I do not doubt that the brethren & sisters who voted for the taking down of the house, did what they then thought best. If they erred, they will probably see their error and mourn over it. Let us not try to increase their grief by our reproaches and especially not by impeaching their motives.

Referring to Hannah's letter of February 25, Whipple responded:

> Oh how I do wish you had never written it. I think I can conceive of how you felt when you heard that the house in which you had lived and labored and prayed and suffered, rejoiced and mourned, was taken down, and your agony at the thought that some of the youth whom you loved and for whose salvation you hoped, some whom you perhaps hoped would be gems in your crown of rejoicing, would be scattered and perhaps stumble and perish upon the dark mountains of sin.
>
> I can understand your apprehension that, in the general removal of the goods etc., valued testimonials from friends never to be seen again in the flesh, precious mementos of departed and sainted fellow laborers or relatives would be lost, or were lost, but that was the time for you to commune with your heart and God and be still. It was not the time for

writing to those who had done these things. Especially was it not the time for reproach. You were too deeply moved to trust your own spirit. You would be in danger of speaking in haste as did David, or unadvised as was Moses.

I think, my dear Sister, that you did both; but I have confidence in you that you will not persist in wrong, nor be offended when kindly, and in a spirit of love, [I]endeavor to point out your error, not for the purpose of increasing your grief, but to comfort you by giving you the opportunity to correct it.

In reference to the "Address" quoted earlier, Whipple wrote:

I wish the brethren and sisters had not written it. I wish that instead of it they had each one written to you in love, beseeching of you to remove the root of bitterness. I think you would have withdrawn it, and apologized for writing it. I fear that their formal "address," signed deliberately by them all, must have pained you greatly, but you must make allowances for them acting as they did under the belief that you meant to accuse them of all these things; make allowances for them even as you would wish to have them make allowances for you when you wrote to them.

In other words, Whipple wanted the missionaries to follow the "Golden Rule." But that was not easy for Hannah—not only was she emotionally drained, but she was physically worn out as well. Indeed, she talked about dying in Africa and was convinced that she would not live to return to the United States. Hannah decided to take the advice of a doctor in Freetown, who told her that her health had worsened and confirmed her fear that she might not live if she remained in Africa. Without the permission of the American Missionary Association, she booked passage on the same ship as George Thompson which was to sail for the United States on April 1, 1856.

Shortly before leaving, Hannah wrote a poem (partially quoted earlier) describing the area surrounding the Mission and the many flowers she had raised from seed:

This place to my heart is sacred and dear,
Where our White House stood by the river clear;
Majestic palm-trees wave their tufted plumes,
And roses each month exhale their perfumes.

Here stands the bread-tree, all loaded with fruit;
And guavas, for jellies so much in repute;
Plantains in clusters, so rich to behold,
Bananas, in color like finest gold.

The capsicum grows full six feet in height,
And pepper, used freely by black and white;
The pride of China, and pride of Peru,
With cactus, and limes and bell-flowers blue.

The castor-plant grows for Africa's race free,
For the palma christi is here a tree;
No winter causes its foliage to fall,
Its clusters of beans are free unto all.

Here the cocoa spreads its palmate leaves,
And the mango's dense foliage moves in each breeze;
Its clusters of fruit the branches bend low,
But pawpaws and figs on the tree-trunks grow.

Here cypress-vines choice are trained with care,
With other rich flowers and exotics rare;
And the bright amaranths their luster shed,
With hibiscus florets, purple, white, red.

Here's the pine-apple hedge, with its choice fruit,
And sour and sweet-sop, which ever may suit;
Red cherries quite rare, with acid so fine,
With plums and molasses-fruit, and the grape-vine.

Here oranges grow, and lemons so fair,
Which white hands have planted and pruned with care;
The cashew-nut too, with its velvet-like flowers,
And then periwinkles, which grace eastern bowers.

Arrow-root, cocoa, and ginger grow here,
Esculent roots by the natives held dear;
And okra for soups esteemed very nice,
When used in palaver-sauce, on fine rice.

These gardens inclosed with a hedge of green,
Where sensitive plants and tulips are seen,
And marigolds raise their bright, golden heads,
While portulaccas bloom on their humble beds.

The arbor is graced with passion-flower vines,
And granadilla fruit in its shade reclines;
The sugar-cane too, yields its succulent sweet,
While rice, and cassava, and fine yams they eat.

Here are trees, plants, and flowers, too many to name,
For the time has expired I have to remain;
Can any forbid that I drop now a tear,
As I leave to these natives my labors so dear.

And say to this place I have loved so well,
Kaw Mendi, and loved ones, farewell! farewell!
The scenes though to me they are dear as an eye
I say to you all, goodby! goodby!

The captain is waiting, and oarsmen too,
To row me far hence in the mission canoe;
So farewell, Kaw Mendi—Oh, farewell to you,
True friends, well-beloved, my parting adieu.

While Dr. Lee was undoubtedly glad to see them leave, he still found it necessary to protest Thompson's decision to take two African boys home with him and wrote to Rev. Whipple:

Should Mr. Thompson return and take the boys with him as he calculated when he left here, it will be on his own account. While we think it well for them to go, we do not think it propper (sic) for him to take them. Charles Jones is not an apt schollar (sic) but may make a good mechanic. Thomas Tucker is a lazy boy of good mind and tallent (sic) he is young yet and may overcome his indolence.

Thompson obviously didn't agree and made the necessary arrangements for the two boys to make the voyage. There was some discussion about valid passports, and passage expenses. Lee wrote to Whipple at the time that he expected the boys to be smuggled out, but as it turned out they worked on board to pay for their passage.

Lee's prediction that the two boys would never profit from an American education was disproved. Thomas De Sallier Tucker graduated from Oberlin College in 1865 and went on to become a lawyer. He was engaged in editorial work for some time in the South and was president of the State Normal School of Florida for five years. Charles Jones graduated from Oberlin College with a divinity degree and ministered to a church in Mississippi.

Thompson, after eight years in Africa, decided to retire from foreign missionary work. He moved to Oberlin, Ohio, for a time and then went to Northern Michigan in 1860, where he was involved in home missionary work for nearly twenty years.

Hannah, on the other hand, was not ready to forsake missionary work despite poor health and her feelings of betrayal and abandonment. She wrote:

> I doubt not, under God, I owe my life to the sea voyage on my way to this country. That is not only my opinion but the opinion expressed by the friends who saw me at Westford, some of whom expressed the opinion that my health was ruined for any Country. I do not myself doubt, had I remained in Africa, I should ere this have died of the Liver Complaint from which I had been suffering severely for the last three years at the mission. I had been teaching some time when I could scarce hold up my aching head and as soon as through taken my couch too sick for any employ. I suppose from pathology a new liver has now formed, as the extreme pain in my side no longer keeps me from sleep at night.

On November 27, 1856, Hannah received a letter from George Whipple which gave her a much-needed lift. He expressed confidence in her and believed she had the Mission's best interests at heart. She had apparently received a written retraction from George Thompson concerning his signature on the "Address," asking her forgiveness.

Later she learned that the AMA wanted her to return to Africa, but not to Kaw Mendi, although she probably would have accepted a return posting. Even though the Mission House and school had been moved, the Association planned to have some natives stay on with perhaps one missionary in charge. Hannah was given the opportunity to decide whether she wanted to take on that responsibility or continue to teach at another location.

The Association was not quick to respond to Hannah's letters in which she said she preferred to labor among the natives rather than the missionaries. "I would, by all means, prefer being located at a station with native helpers or not more than one Missionary, and I still give it as my opinion, founded on experience, that Missionaries should ever be scattered among the natives, leaving merely enough to direct at the station where native helpers are to be obtained who are qualified for the work."

She spent the next year convalescing in Union and visiting her relatives. By the fall of 1857, she felt well enough to enroll in a course of medical lectures at Oberlin College where she lived with George Thompson and his family until 1859.

Convinced that the Lord had work for her to do in Kentucky, Hannah next headed south across the Ohio River, praying at each train and stage stop that God would reveal His will for her. At Harrodsburg, she met an innkeeper from Maxville (now Macksville) who was looking for an "Eastern teacher." Obviously qualified, she began a two-year stint as principal of a female seminary there. Hannah, however, was caught on the horns of a dilemma: she desperately needed a paying position, but this position conflicted with her long-held conviction about the evils of slavery. She described her feelings in a letter to Rev. George Whipple dated December 10, 1860:

> My sympathies are not in common with a slaveholding community though I read their publications and know much more of southern pride, caste, et cetera, than formerly. Killing a person is not considered so dangerous as circulating incendiary publications such as *Helper's Impending Crisis, The American Missionary*, etc. The former I have never seen, and the latter I receive very irregularly.... First, after perusing them, I presented them to some pupils, till I was told they were incendiary and recommended to gather them in and burn them, as they might be the means of imprisoning me. This I have not done, though I do not feel the same liberty to circulate them now for a native of Kentucky has been a long time in the county jail for having the Impending Crisis.
>
> When I am accused of reading incendiary matter, I reply you allow your children & friends to read plenty of novels and romances which all consider wanting in truthful statements with impunity, granting that privilege—saying you do not compel them to endorse the sentiment—may not I read with the same liberation?

After the execution of the radical abolitionist, John Brown, it was unsafe for other abolitionists in the South. Hannah decided it was time to leave Kentucky and crossed the Ohio River into Ohio, which was a free state. While in Ohio, she wrote "My Bible Views of Slavery," in which she cited her reasons, based on the Bible, for believing that Blacks were not an inferior race as they were being portrayed.

She wrote: "[I]s it not surprising that our blessed Savior should have Simon the Canaanite as one of the twelve apostles he ordained and sent out, if the prevailing sentiment in this country that the negroes are an inferior race, be true." Referring to Abraham Lincoln who had just been elected, she continued:

> Even the Southerners allow that the Canaanites were black and our next President, a white Kentuckian by birth, does not think them competent to hold office in the United States.
>
> I would beg leave of permission to refer him to black Solomon, the wisest man; the king of Israel, who was the son of Bathsheba, the black wife of David.... If you look at the cabinet of David and Solomon you will find black men among the counselors (sic) and men of power.

At a time when women were expected to keep their opinions to themselves, Hannah's views could not have been popular among her contemporaries, but that did not deter her either then or later.

# Chapter Five: Hannah Meets a Sabbath-keeping Adventist

Hannah returned to Connecticut to prepare herself for what she hoped would be another term of service in West Africa. It was here she first became aware of Sabbath-keeping Adventists through contact with Stephen Haskell, a prominent leader of New England believers, whom she met while he was visiting in Woodstock, Connecticut, in late 1861 or early 1862. Haskell gave her several tracts and a copy of J. N. Andrews's *History of the Sabbath*, a book she clearly treasured and frequently recommended to others. Although she read the tracts carefully, she did not make any immediate decision to change her church affiliation.

**Rev. Stephen Haskell**
Taken from "Seventh-day Adventists in the South Pacific," by Noel Clapham et al., 1985

Instead, in 1862, with no prospects for employment as a missionary under the auspices of the AMA, Hannah again sailed for Africa, this time to Liberia, "deeply impressed that there was a special opening for me." She learned that there was a vacancy at a Mission Station on the St. Paul River near Monrovia. One of the teachers had become ill, and Hannah, certain that her prayers were being answered, accepted the temporary position. A few months later, she was offered a management position at the Hoffman Mission

School at Cape Palmas which was essentially an orphan asylum. Rev. Hoffman, director of the Hoffman Mission School, was a pioneer in working with blind and disabled children, having devised a form of raised type that was later invented by Braille.

An article by Stephen Haskell titled, "Tract and Missionary Work," and printed in the *Advent Review and Sabbath Herald* in December of 1872, stated that Hannah was in charge of the mission, "acting the part of preacher, teacher, physician, general provider, and in fact, the general civilizer of a company of natives gathered at the mission."

Haskell was indefatigable in his efforts to convince Hannah that she should become a Seventh-day Adventist. He made arrangements to have the *Advent Review and Sabbath Herald* (now the *Adventist Review*) sent to her in Africa, along with various related publications. Hannah's intense study of the Bible as well as the literature sent by Haskell led her to believe that the seventh day was clearly meant to be Saturday and convinced a fellow missionary in the process. The fact that the Adventists celebrated the Sabbath on Saturday was only one aspect of what attracted Hannah to this new religious group. Seventh-day Adventists, from their earliest days, actively sought freedom for all and worked toward abolition of slavery as well as roles for women in the church, and they fostered a strong opposition to formalized church creeds. Freedom was also emphasized through an orientation toward temperance and health reform. Proper care of the physical body would yield a clear mind with which to perceive scriptural truths. These were clearly ideas that appealed to Hannah and set her apart from her Congregational brethren who, at the time, were much more restrictive in their beliefs, especially concerning the submissive role of women in the church.

Her first letter from Africa to the *Review* was published in the March 29, 1864, edition: "I do not know of any others on the Coast who keep the Seventh-day," she wrote, "but that is no proof against its authenticity. I only wonder that many good people reject the commandments of God by their traditions." While she had not yet been baptized into the new denomination, she continued: "Your people may now consider that you have a wholehearted Seventh-day Adventist here, waiting with you for that blessed appearing of Him who we love and adore, and purpose to worship evermore."

A second letter to the *Review and Herald* dated October 12, 1864, reported:

> I feel quite lonely keeping the Sabbath by myself. I hope your society
> may do something toward a Sabbath-keeping mission in this part of

Africa. I do not wonder there has not been a greater outpouring of the Spirit, when I think of the follies which have been set against the eternal truth of God. Oh, that the time might be hastened when all God's people shall see eye to eye. I love the truth, and by it hope to be made free indeed. Till then I must labor in that slot allotted me by a wise providence and may I so labor that God's blessing may ever attend and crown my efforts with abundant success. I ask no higher boon than to be wise to win souls. I know that God can perfect strength even through my weakness and in him I will put my trust, and on him cast my care. I know not what awaits me, but leaning on his potent arm I am safe.

By early 1865, Hannah was again teaching among the Mendi people at the Good Hope Mission in Sierra Leone. Within months she answered an urgent appeal to manage another orphan asylum, this time in Freetown. The growing tension between Hannah's belief in Adventism and the traditional Protestant views of her Mission Board is shown in the following lines of poetry by Hannah printed in the January 9, 1866, *Advent Review and Sabbath Herald:*

> Those who deemed His coming near
> Saying Christ would soon appear,
> Have been wild fanatics called,
> Scorned and mocked by great and small.

An editorial note in the same edition indicated that Hannah was "at the risk of losing her position as a missionary teacher." On February 13, 1866, the *Review* printed her next letter, which was probably written in early December 1865, stating that the separation from her Mission Board because of her new beliefs had already occurred. "They ... deem it expedient to send a principal to fill the position I now occupy.... I may visit America next spring, unless there should, in the providence of God, be a special opening for me."

Hannah's health had continued to deteriorate during her second African tour. She described herself as worn down by "fever, heart disease, and liver complaint," noting that her physician had told her she must return to the United States if she expected to live. She wrote of the extraordinary events leading up to her voyage:

> Quite a number of deaths had occurred in the harbor at Freetown. While I was at the Mission House, waiting for sailing after my passage was engaged, our missionary physician had died, and the missionary at whose house I was, buried his only son. The next day I was informed that the flag of the "Chanticleer" was at half mast, and the hearse passed

the Mission House with the remains of the Supercargo. I felt truly sad and perplexed not knowing what to do, but prayed the Lord to guide me aright.

My mission friends advised me to decline going on that ship, and I wrote the Captain to that intent, but he assured me it was overwork that brought on the African fever and caused the sudden death, and no contagion need be apprehended as the ship had been thoroughly fumigated with disinfecting agents, and repainted, adding in the words of inspiration, 'Though I walk through the valley of the shadow of death, I will fear no evil for Thou art with me.'

Brother C. said he admired the spirit of the letter, and we decided that missionaries should be no less courageous than sea captains. I was accommodated on that trading vessel only in consequence of being a missionary who needed a change to recruit health. I had been refused passage on three vessels previous to this. One of them, the *Africa*, had with difficulty returned to port, and was now having her cargo re-shipped on the Chanticleer, her damages on the shoals having unfitted her, so that she was condemned as unseaworthy; and I saw that the good hand of the Lord was in it, that she would not take me as a passenger.

Another, the Ann Elizabeth, whose captain would not wait for me to go on board, though his accommodations were good, ran into, and sank a ship near Boston Harbor, and the captain was being tried for it, when he reached Boston; and our pilot informed us that he had been previously tried for flogging one of his men in such an inhuman manner as to cause his death.

I was thankful I was not permitted to be on board such a ship, to witness the cry of drowning persons; as the collision was so sudden it admitted of no escape. All went down to a watery grave. I had a safe passage through the mercy of God, though two of our seamen found a grave beneath the ocean's billows.

Arriving in Boston in late spring, she then traveled to South Lancaster, Massachusetts, located forty miles west of the city, where she worshipped with the small Adventist group there and was later baptized as a Seventh-day Adventist.

She wrote: "I was glad to unite with the little church there in keeping the commands of God and the faith of Jesus. This privilege I had long desired."[40]

After witnessing a healing service while in South Lancaster, Hannah requested that she also be anointed. The simple service was held at Haskell's home, and Hannah described herself as "healed," noting "I have not enjoyed so good health for years."[41]

Hannah resided with relatives in Connecticut for the balance of 1866 and the first half of 1867. Letters reprinted in the *Review,*[42] which she had written to a cousin and a nephew during these months, indicate that she was vigorously defending her Adventist beliefs despite family criticism.

> I was necessarily delayed in writing to you last month, as I was ill, and with difficulty able to write my sister, and English correspondents. They regret my Sabbath views, and say that as the first day has been kept so many centuries, it is strange I should be doubting on that point. They say it was kept by the apostles, and quote Paul's sermon on the first day of the week as proof conclusive.

> I wrote them how futile seemed their arguments and that instead of proof, it was doubtless a Saturday evening meeting, and that Paul set out on his journey Sunday morning. They desired to see the book which I spoke of on the Sabbath, and I forwarded it to them, hoping and praying it might prove a blessing to them, and requesting them when they had read it, to forward it to Rev. Geo. Muller of Bristol Orphan Houses.

Seeking to find God's will through prayers and meditation, Hannah decided to undertake the nine hundred mile trip by train to Battle Creek, then the largest center of Seventh-day Adventists in the world, with the hope of finding employment and fellowship there. Because she had kept in touch with the Adventist church through its weekly publication, *The Review and Herald,* she was very much aware of the activities of this group and thought she would find a haven there.

She arrived in early summer of 1867 and quite by accident met Sister Strong, who was also new to the area but had Adventist friends there. Sister Strong tried,

---

40   Hannah More to editor, *Advent Review and Sabbath Herald,* 28, No. 16, September 18, 1866

41   Ibid

42   Hannah More to editor, *Advent Review and Sabbath Herald,* 27, February 13, 1866

unsuccessfully, to find employment for Hannah as well as a place to stay. The Health Reform Institute gave Hannah free room and board for a few days; one Adventist family boarded her for two days, another for four. But it soon became painfully clear to Hannah and Sister Strong that no Adventist families in Battle Creek were willing to open their homes to the teacher/missionary whose clothing "was not just such as would meet the approval of the eye of taste and fashion." This leads to further speculation that it may not have been just her unfashionable clothing that led to their lack of hospitality, but perhaps it was her physical appearance, since she wore concave glasses which magnified her eyes, one of which was blind and unfocused.

Ellen White, who was away when Hannah arrived, was livid when she learned that none of her people were willing to accommodate Hannah for more than one or two days at a time and that Hannah, bewildered by the cold, indifferent treatment she encountered and not knowing where to turn, contacted her old friend and associate, Rev. George Thompson, who was then living in Leland, Michigan. Traveling by rail to Chicago, Hannah borrowed money from friends there and went by ship up Lake Michigan to Leland, arriving in midsummer.

Because she was happy to be reunited with George and Martha Thompson, and more than willing to pay her way by teaching Thompson's children and helping Martha with the household chores, she did not feel she could complain about her windowless room in the attic, even though it was hot in the summer and extremely cold in the winter.

Thompson made it clear that he did not want her to impose her beliefs on his family. She could celebrate her Sabbath (Saturday) in her room while they, of course, would attend the Presbyterian Church on Sunday. But Hannah was not to be deterred and continued to hope that he would

> yet embrace the holy Sabbath. Sister Thompson does believe in it already. He is wonderfully set in his ways, and of course thinks he is right. Could I only get him to read the books I brought, the History of the Sabbath, etc., but he looks at them and calls them infidel, and says they seem to him to carry error in their front, when if they would only read carefully each sentiment of our tenets, I can but think they would embrace them as Bible truths and see their beauty and consistency. I doubt not but that Sister T. would be glad to immediately become a Seventh-day Adventist were it not that her husband is so bitterly opposed to any such thing.[43]

---

43   Hannah More letter to James White, August 29, 1867

Even though she was a Seventh-day Adventist, she did not hesitate to accept an opportunity to preach on Sundays when Thompson realized, due to other commitments, he would be unable to keep his church appointments in Leland. However, he warned her, "You are not to make your peculiar beliefs prominent. Believe them yourself, if you must; but don't spread any heresy among my people."

In what is believed to be Hannah's last letter written to James White on February 20, 1868, she talks of her "delicate state of health":

> It does not seem possible for me to get to you till spring comes. The roads are bad enough without snow. They tell me my best way is to wait until navigation opens, then go to Milwaukee, and thence to Grand Haven, to take the railroad to the point nearest your place. I had hoped to get among our dear people last fall, but was not permitted the privilege. I wish I could get to you, but it seems impossible—in my delicate state of health to set out alone on such a journey in the depth of winter....

> I think my health has suffered from keeping the Sabbath alone in my chamber, in the cold; but I did not think I could keep it where all manner of work and worldly conversation was the order of the day.... I think it is the most laborious working day with those who keep the first day.... Oh how I long to be again with Sabbath keepers!

> Sister White will want to see me in the reform dress. Will she be so kind as to send me a pattern, and I will pay her when I get among you. I like it much. Sister Thompson thinks she would like to wear the reform dress.[44]

> I have had a difficulty in breathing, so that I have not been able to sleep for more than a week occasioned, I suppose, by the stovepipe's parting and completely filling my room with smoke and gas at bedtime, and my sleeping there without proper ventilation. I did not, at the time, suppose smoke was so unwholesome, nor consider that the impure gas which generated from the wood and coal was mingled with it. I awoke with such a sense of suffocation that I could not breathe lying down, and spent the remainder of the night sitting up. I never before knew the dreadful feeling of stifling sensations. I began to fear I should never sleep again. I therefore resigned myself into the hands of

---

44    She never got the opportunity to wear the reform dress which, it turned out, never became popular among the female Adventists. Even the men expressed disapproval. The length of the skirt was shortened by about six inches and pantaloons were worn underneath.

God for life or death, entreating Him to spare me if He had any further need of me.... I felt entirely reconciled to the hand of God upon me. But I also felt that satanic influences must be resisted. I, therefore, bade Satan get behind me and told the Lord that I would not turn my hand over to choose either life or death.... Life is of no account to me, so far as its pleasures are concerned. I would not live uselessly to be a mere blot or blank in life. And though it seems a martyr's death to die thus, I am resigned if that is God's will.

She died eleven days later, succumbing to "congestion of the stomach." Her funeral was attended by people of many faiths; Thompson, her longtime friend, preached the sermon.

The following quotation is from a letter dated March 4, 1868, written by George Thompson, to George Whipple, Secretary of the AMA at the time of Hannah's death:

You will be painfully interested to know that Miss Hannah More, so long your missionary in Africa, died in my house this week and was buried yesterday. She had expected to leave in the Spring for a place further South, but God had other work for her "up higher." Our long winter was too much for her tropical constitution. For a number of weeks she was quite unwell by night—could not breathe easily, nor sleep.

The last four days she suffered night and day very much, but was quiet in mind, willing ready and anxious to die—even here in this out of the way place—often prayed for deliverance. Repeated very many passages of scripture expressive of strong faith and submission—often exclaimed 'God is good,' and near her last said 'Into Thy hands I commit my spirit, for time and eternity.'

We buried her yesterday. All classes came to her funeral—a large crowd and I preached from one of her expressions "To be with God which is far better."'

It was thought, at the time, that this might be a temporary burial and that Hannah's fellow believers would want to bury her permanently near church headquarters in Battle Creek. Others speculated that her family might want to have her remains moved to Union, but that was not the case. Instead, she was buried in a grave in the middle of the Porter plot, apparently between John Porter and his wife, in the Concord Burying Ground.

Ellen White, one of founders of the Seventh-day Adventist Church, wrote:

Poor Sister More! When we heard that she was dead, my husband felt terrible. We both felt as though a dear mother, for whose society our very hearts yearned, was no more. Some may say, "if we had stood in the place of those who knew something of this sister's wishes and wants, we would not have done as they did." I hope you will never have to suffer the stings of conscience which some must feel who were so interested in their own affairs as to be unwilling to bear any responsibility in her case. May God pity those who are so afraid of deception as to neglect a worthy, self-sacrificing servant of Christ. The remark was made as an excuse for this neglect. We have been bitten so many times that we are afraid of strangers. Did our Lord and His disciples instruct us to be very cautious and not entertain strangers, lest we should possibly make some mistake and get bitten by having the trouble of caring for an unworthy person?

**Tombstone reads:**

**In Memory of Hannah More, Missionary
to Africa. Aged fifty-nine years and three
months. To be with Christ is far better. Phil. 1:23**
Photo courtesy of Rev. William Knott

Sister Hannah More is dead, and died a martyr to the selfishness of a people who profess to be seeking for glory, honor, immortality, and eternal life. Exiled from believers during the past cold winter, this self-sacrificing missionary died because no heart was bountiful enough to receive her. I blame no one. I am not judge.[45]

Rev. William Knott, a Seventh-day Adventist, wrote about Hannah in *A Winter's Tale—The tragic case of Hannah More*, saying: "Ellen White clearly saw in Hannah's story, not just a pathetic tale of neglect and mistreatment, but the slighting of one of God's chief servants for the infant church." Thus Hannah became a symbol for the Adventists, that the neglect of Hannah was the neglect of Jesus in her person and that this should never be allowed to happen again.

> She carried the light with her, and left works on present truth at every missionary station on the African shore.... The Orphan Asylum, in Bristol, England, under the management of Mr. Muller, author of "Muller's Life and Trust," has received the History of the Sabbath and other publications through the instrumentality of Hannah More. A trail of light has marked her track from Africa to the British Isles; from the New England States to Northern Michigan, where she found her quiet resting place to await the day of rewards, when she will see the result of a life devoted to missionary labor. She scattered the light of present truth into at least four distinct nations.

Hannah would undoubtedly be amazed that after 130 years she is still remembered both by residents of Connecticut and by the Adventists. Described in a brief biography in the *History of Union, Connecticut*[46] as a "woman of great ability, and of a noble and devoted Christian character," she was all that and more, courageous, indefatigable, spirited, and multitalented. She gave her all to what she believed was a righteous cause: saving the souls of Native American and African children and adults so that they might have eternal life. She was truly "Tuesday's child full of grace."

---

45   *Testimonies for the Church*, Vol. I, by Ellen G. White, Pacific Press Publishing Assoc., CA 1948

46   Lawson, Rev. Harvey and Hammond, Charles, *History of Union, Connecticut*, New Haven, CT 1893

# SELECTED BIBLIOGRAPHY

1. Adger, J. B. *Christian Missions in African Colonies*. South Carolina: Steam Power Press of E. H. Britton. 1857.

2. American Missionary, Vol. 49, Issue 3, March 3, 1895.

3. American Missionary Association, Oberlin. *The Mendi Mission in West Africa*, November 10, 1852.

4. "Annual Reports of the American Missionary Association,"1849–69, American Missionary Association, New York.

5. Author unknown. "Africans of the Amistad—Love of Home," *Advent Review and Sabbath Herald*, Vol. XXVII, No. 16, January 9, 1866.

6. Author unknown. "Blacks Should Accompany Mendi on Return to Sierra Leone," *African Repository and Colonial Journal*, Vol. XVII, No. 22, November 11, 1841.

7. Barber, John W. *History of the Amistad Captives*. Connecticut: Hitchcock & Stafford Printers. 1840.

8. Barr, Robert, Secretary Oberlin College, letter addressed to Wilbur H. Oda of Barto, PA, October 1, 1952: contains a short biographical sketch of George Thompson.

9. Bartlett, S. C. *Sketches of the Missions of the American Board*. Boston: Eerdsman's Publishing Co. 1872.

10. Beardsley, Rev. N. B. letter to Rev. David Green, October 10, 1840, Union, Connecticut. In American Board of Commissioners for Foreign Missions, Houghton Library.

11. Butrick, D. Letters from Mount Zion to Rev. David Greene, January 15, May 22, and July 30, 1844.

12. Cable, Mary. *Black Odyssey, the Case of the Slave Ship Amistad.* New York: Viking Press. 1971.

13. Campbell, O. B. *Mission to the Cherokees.* Metro Press, Oklahoma City, Oklahoma, 1971.

14. Catalogue of the Trustees, Instructors & Students of Monson Academy for the year ending August 11, 1840, Merriam Wood and Co., Printers, Springfield, Massachusetts, 1840.

15. Clapham, Noel et al., "Seventh-day Adventists in the South Pacific, 1885–1985," Signs Publishing, Warburton, Victoria, Australia, 1985.

16. Chamberlain, Rev. William. Letters to Rev. D. Greene, January and September 12, 1838.

17. *Connecticut Missionary* #25, November 6, 1868. Hannah More obituary.

18. Records of Congregational Church of Union, Conn, 1789–1922. Connecticut State Library. Connecticut.

19. Curtiss, George. *History of the Congregational Church of Union, Connecticut.* Connecticut: Burroughs & Hopkins. 1914.

20. Dana, Robert. *American Women in Mission: A Social History of Their Thought and Practice.* Georgia: Mercer University Press. 1996.

21. Davis, Susan. *I was a Stranger: The Story of Jesus in the Person of Hannah More.* California: Pacific Press Pub. Assoc. 1979.

22. Day, Kellog. Letter from Dwight Mission to Rev. Green, September 4, 1845. Houghton Library. Boston.

23. DeBoer, Clara Merritt. *Be Jubilant My Feet: African American Abolitionists in the American Missionary Association 1839–1861.* New York: Garland Publishing, Inc. 1994.

24. Dodge, R. L. Letter from the Dwight Mission, Oklahoma, to Rev. D. Greene, July 23, 1841. Yale University Library, New Haven, Connecticut.

25. Drury, A. W. *History of the Church of the United Brethren in Christ.* Dayton: Otterbein Press. 1924.

26. Editorial, "Mendi Mission," *Oberlin Evangelist*, Vol. VII, No. 23, November 5, 1845.

27. Flickinger, D. K., Rev. Wm. McKeen. *History of the Origin, Development and Condition of Missions among the Sherbro & Mendi Tribes in Western Africa.* Ohio: United Brethern Publishing House. 1885.

28. Gaustad, Edwin S. *The Rise of Adventism: Religion and Society in Mid-Nineteenth Century America.* New York: Harper and Row. 1974.

29. Glimpses of West Africa with Sketches of Missionary Life, New York, American Tract Society. 1865.

30. Graham, Thomas John, *Modern Domestic Medicine, To which is Added, a Domestic Materia Medica.* London. 1827.

31. Green, Rev. David. Letter to J. Hitchcock dated February 26, 1844. Yale University Library, New Haven, Connecticut.

32. Haskell, S. N. "Tract and Missionary Work," *Advent Review and Sabbath Herald,* Vol. 41, No. 1, dated December 17, 1872.

33. Heard, Edward F., "Dwight Mission Under the American Board." PhD diss., University of Tulsa, 1958.

34. Hitchcock, J. Letter to Rev. David Green, Missionary House, Boston, Massachusetts, June 3, 1841. Houghton Library, Boston, Massachusetts.

35. Hosford, Mary Eliza. Letter from Oberlin, Ohio, dated August 24, 1931 concerning George Thompson. Oberlin College, Oberlin, Ohio.

36. Johnson, Clifton Herman, "The American Missionary Association, 1846–1861: A Study of Christian Abolitionism." PhD diss., University of North Carolina at Chapel Hill, 1958.

37. Jones, Howard. "Mutiny on the Amistad: All We Want Is Make Us Free." The Connecticut Scholar, Occasional Papers of the Connecticut Humanities Council, 1992.

38. Keller, Charles Roy. *The Second Great Awakening in Connecticut.* Connecticut: Yale University Press. 1942.

39. Koesler-Grack, Rachel A., *Captain John Ross,* Heinemann Library, Chicago. 2004.

40. Knott, Rev. William. *A Winter's Tale, Adventist Review,* January 22, 1998.

41. Larned, Ellen D. *History of Windham County, Connecticut*, Volumes I and II. Ellen D. Larned. 1874.

42. Lawson, Ellen NicKenzie with Marlene D. Merrill. *The Three Sarahs, Studies in Women and Religion*, Vol. 13, The Edwin Mellen Press, New York and Toronto. 1984.

43. Harvey M. Lawson and Charles Hammond. *History of Union, Connecticut.* Connecticut: Press of Price, Lee and Adkins. 1893.

44. Little, Kenneth. *The Mende of Sierra Leone: A West African People in Transition.* London: Routledge and Kegan Paul. 1951.

45. Lyon, Mary. *Mary Lyon and the Mount Holyoke Missionaries.* New York: Oxford University Press. 1997.

46. Marr, Warren, "Out of Bondage." *United Church Herald*, 1964.

47. McLoughlin, William G. *Cherokees and Missionaries, 1789–1839.* New Haven: Yale University Press. 1984.

48. McLoughlin, William G. *After the Trail of Tears: the Cherokee's Struggle for Sovereignty; 1839–1880.* Chapel Hill: University of North Carolina Press. 1993.

49. "The Mendian Negroes," *Advent Review and Herald of the Sabbath*, Vol. 41, No. 1, December 17, 1841.

50. Merrill, Marlene. "Sarah Margru Kinson: An Amistad Captive Comes to Oberlin." Talk presented at Oberlin Inn, Ohio, April 8, 1988.

51. *Missionary Herald*, American Board of Commissioners for Foreign Mission, Boston: published for the Board by Samuel T. Armstrong 1821–1934 (researched monthly publications from 1840–1850) at Yale Divinity School on microfilm.

52. Monson Historical Society, *History of Monson, Massachusetts*, compiled by Monson Historical Society. 1960.

53. Moore, Hannah. Letter to Secretaries of the American Board of Commissioners for Foreign Missions, October 1, 1838. In American Board of Commissioners for Foreign Missions, Houghton Library.

54. Moore, Hannah. Letter from Dwight Cherokee Nation to Rev. Mr. Greene, Oct. 20, 1841. In American Board of Commissioners for Foreign Missions, Houghton Library.

55. Moore, Hannah. Letter from Dwight Mission to Rev. Mr. Greene, March 30, 1842. In American Board of Commissioners for Foreign Missions, Houghton Library.

56. Moore, Hannah. Letter from Dwight Mission to sisters Joanna and Amy, and Hannah's mother with notes from three Cherokee Indian children, April 4, 1842, Sturbridge Village Library, Sturbridge, Massachusetts.

57. Moore, Hannah. Letter from Dwight to Rev. D. Greene, July 14, 1842. In American Board of Commissioners for Foreign Missions, Houghton Library.

58. Moore, Hannah. Letter from Dwight Mission to Rev. Mr. Green, August 4, 1842. In American Board of Commissioners for Foreign Missions, Houghton Library.

59. Moore, Hannah. Letter from Dwight Mission to Rev. Green, March 20, 1843. In American Board of Commissioners for Foreign Missions, Houghton Library.

60. Moore, Hannah. Letter from Africa undated, *Advent Review and Sabbath Herald*, No. 155, October 11, 1864.

61. Moore, Hannah. Letter undated, *Advent Review and Sabbath Herald*, Vol. XXV, September 18, 1866.

62. Moore, Hannah. Letter from Dwight Mission to Rev. Green, June 4, 1845. In American Board of Commissioners for Foreign Missions, Houghton Library.

63. Moore, Hannah. Letter from Dwight Mission to "much respected friend," September 10, 1845. In American Board of Commissioners for Foreign Missions, Houghton Library.

64. Moore, Hannah. Letter from Willington, Connecticut to Rev. Green, June 11, 1849. In American Board of Commissioners for Foreign Missions, Houghton Library.

65. Moore, Hannah. Letter from Mendi Mission, West Africa, addressed to Sisters Eldridge in Willington, Connecticut, August 31, 1852, Willington Historical Society Collections, Willington, Connecticut.

66. Moore, Hannah. Letter from Mendi Mission to Mr. Harned, October 12, 1852. In American Missionary Association.

67. Moore, Hannah. Letter to Rev. George Whipple, March 20, 1857. In American Missionary Association.

68. Moore, Hannah. Poem, "I Say Unto All, Watch," *Advent Review and Sabbath Herald,* Vol. XXV, January 9, 1866.

69. Moore, Hannah. Letter undated, *Advent Review and Sabbath Herald,* No. 10, February 11 and 18, 1868.

70. Nettles, Tom. *Asahel Nettleton: Sermons from the Second Great Awakening.* Iowa: International Outreach, Inc. 1995.

71. Numbers, Ronald L. *Prophetess of Health: A Study of Ellen G. White.* New York: Harper and Row. 1976.

72. Orr, J. Letter from Dwight Mission to Rev. D. Green, May 10, 1847. In American Board of Commissioners for Foreign Missions, Houghton Library.

73. Betty Payne and Oscar Payne. *Dwight: A Brief History of Old Dwight Cherokee Mission 1820–1953.* Presbyterian Mission, Tulsa, Oklahoma, 1954.

74. Pesci, David, *Amistad: The Thunder of Freedom.* New York: Marlowe and Co. 1997.

75. Raymond, Rev. William, "Report on the Mendi Mission; and an Address to the Christian Public in Behalf of Anti-slavery Missions," S. W. Benedict & Co., New York. 1843.

76. Raymond, Rev. William, "Mendi Mission," *Oberlin Evangelist,* Vol. VII, No. 23, November 5, 1845.

77. Reports of the American Board of Commissioners for Foreign Missions, 1841–1850.

78. "Return to Africa," *African Repository and Colonial Journal,* Vol. XVIII, No. 8, June 1, 1841.

79. Strong, J. S. Letter to the AMA dated March 21, 1848, *Home Proceedings,* October, 1848, pgs. 344–350.

80. Thompson, George, Letter to George Whipple, May 24, 1855. In American Board of Commissioners for Foreign Missions, Houghton Library.

81. Thompson, George. Brief information about George Thompson written by his daughter Mrs. Rosa Terboroh, April 28, 1933. In Oberlin College Archives, Oberlin, Ohio.

82. Thompson, George, "To All Christians," *Oberlin Evangelist*, Vol. XI, December 5, 1849.

83. Thompson, George, letter dated June 29, 1848, *Oberlin Evangelist*, Vol. X, No. 18, September 27, 1848.

84. Thompson, George. Obituary in *Oberlin News*, February 9, 1893.

85. Thompson, George. *The Palm Land or West Africa*. London: Dawsons of Pall Mall. 1969.

86. Thompson, George. Biographical sketch in the *Congregational Year Book*, 1894, pg. 37.

87. Thompson, George. Transcript of examination of George Thompson with a view to his ordination, April 6, 1848, Oberlin College, Ohio.

88. Thompson, George. Letter from Kaw Mendi Mission addressed to Editor of *Oberlin Evangelist*, July 20, 1855.

89. Thompson, George. *Thompson in Africa*. Ohio: George Thompson. 1859.

90. Thompson, George. *Africa in a Nutshell*. Ohio: George Thompson. 1881.

91. Thompson, George. *Letters to Sabbath-School Children on Africa, Volumes I through V*. Ohio: American Reform Tract and Book Society. 1858.

92. Thompson, Martha C. Obituary in *Oberlin Tribune*, March 9, 1917.

93. Union, Connecticut Vital Records, 1734–1850, Town Clerk's Office, Union, Connecticut.

94. Upson, Jeannine M., ed. *Union Lands, A People's History*. Massachusetts: Blatchley's Printers. 1984.

95. Washburn, Rev. Cephas. *Reminiscences of the Indians,* Presbyterian Committee of Publication, Johnson Reprint Corporation, New York, London, 1971.

96. Washburn, Rev. Cephas. Letter to Rev. D. Green, August 12, 1839. In the American Board of Commissioners for Foreign Missions at Houghton Library.

97. Washburn, Rev. Cephas. Partial copy of letter from Dwight Mission to Rev. Mr. Green, November 10, 1840. In the American Board of Commissioners for Foreign Missions at the Houghton Library.

98. Washburn, Rev. Cephas. Letter undated (circa 1840), In the American Board of Commissioners for Foreign Missions at Houghton Library.

99. Welter, Barbara. "She Hath Done What She Could: Protestant Women's Missionary Careers in 19th Century America." In *Women in American Religion*, in Janet Wilson James, ed. *Women in American Religion*. University of Pennsylvania Press. 1980.

100. Whipple, Rev. George, "Mendi Mission," *Oberlin Evangelist,* Vol. XI, No. 17, August 15, 1849.

101. White, Ellen G. *Testimonies for the Church, Volumes One and Two*. California: Pacific Press Publishing. 1948.

102. White, James. Letter dated Feb. 11, 1868, *Advent Review and Sabbath Herald,* No. 10, February 18, 1868.

103. Whiton, August Sherril. *The Whiton Family in America, The Genealogy of the Descendents of Thomas Whiton (1635)*. Whiton Family Association, Inc. 1932.

104. Willey, Rev. Worcester. *Among the Cherokees*. Brown, Thurston and Co., Portland, Maine. 1888.

105. Woodward, Grace Steele. *The Cherokees*. Oklahoma: University of Oklahoma Press. 1936.

106. Worcester, S. A. Letter to Rev. Green, Sec., American Board of Commissioners for Foreign Missions dated April 10, 1842. In the American Board of Commissioners for Foreign Missions at Houghton Library.

107. Worcester, S. A. Letter dated August 4, 1841, *Missionary Herald,* dated January 1842, pgs. 14–18.

# APPENDIX A

George Thompson, Hannah's long-time friend and co-worker, left Leland, Michigan, in 1880 and moved to Oberlin, Ohio, where he continued to preach and write books. His biography, which appeared in the March 3, 1895, *The American Missionary*, is quoted below.

## A PIONEER MISSIONARY IN AFRICA

Rev. George Thompson was early enlisted as a missionary in the Mendi Mission on the west coast of Africa. He had been a most ardent friend of the slave, active in aiding their escape from the house of bondage, and as a consequence had spent five years in the Missouri State Prison. He went to Africa in 1848 under the commission of the American Missionary Association, and proved himself to be remarkably useful. One of his most far-reaching efforts was in the work as a peacemaker. A fierce and unrelenting war had been raging among the tribes around the mission, and this was brought to a close through the wise and persistent efforts of Mr. Thompson. He was chosen umpire for the contending chiefs, and after repeated and wearying excursions, and ten interviews or councils with both parties, he at length succeeded. Then came the joy which peace brings. Warriors met and fell on each other's necks; chiefs, who were for years enemies, now shook hands and embraced each other with the affection of long-separated friends; sisters, wives and daughters, long captives, fell into each other's arms, weeping for joy. A chief's daughter was seen running to embrace her father's feet, a wife hastened to welcome her husband and children, and entire towns were filled with cries of gladness. The beatitude, "Blessed are the peacemakers," belongs to Mr. Thompson.

Ill health at length compelled Mr. Thompson to relinquish the work in Africa, and in 1856 he returned to Oberlin, Ohio, where he spent five years working on his book entitled "Palm Land," and in educating the two boys whom he brought with him from Africa. In 1861 he removed his family to northwestern Michigan, where he labored as a home missionary for eighteen years, being the pastor for fifteen years of a church which he established. He then returned to Oberlin, where he remained until his death in 1893. In all these years Mr. Thompson was a laborious and useful man, actively engaged in awakening the churches to an interest in Africa, in writing his books and educating the children. In his later years, while living in Oberlin, he was abundant in labors in connection with Sunday Schools and feeble churches in Ohio and other states.

# APPENDIX B

**Example of Hannah's handwriting and crosshatching to save paper.**

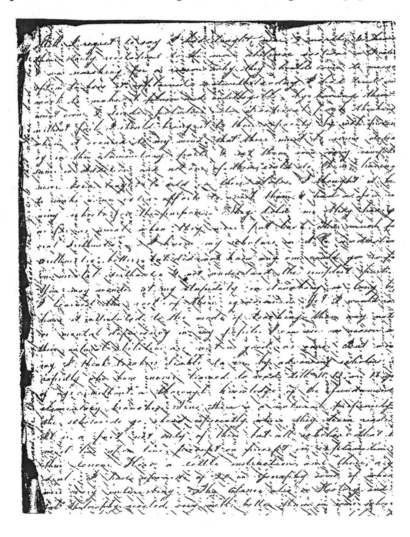

**Pedigree Chart** = C

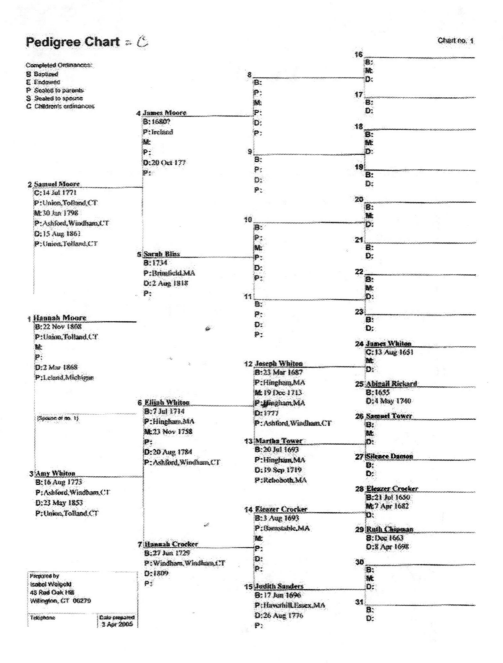

Completed Ordinances:
B Baptized
E Endowed
P Sealed to parents
S Sealed to spouse
C Children's ordinances

16
B:
M:
D:

8
B:
P:
M:

17
B:
D:

4 James Moore
B: 1680?
P: Ireland
M:
P:
D: 20 Oct 177
P:

18
B:
M:
D:

9
B:
P:
D:
P:

19
B:
D:

2 Samuel Moore
C: 14 Jul 1771
P: Union, Tolland, CT
M: 30 Jan 1798
P: Ashford, Windham, CT
D: 15 Aug 1861
P: Union, Tolland, CT

20
B:
M:
D:

10
B:
P:
M:
P:
D:
P:

21
B:
D:

5 Sarah Bliss
B: 1734
P: Brimfield, MA
D: 2 Aug 1818
P:

22
B:
M:
D:

11
B:
P:
D:
P:

23
B:
D:

1 Hannah Moore
B: 22 Nov 1808
P: Union, Tolland, CT
M:
P:
D: 2 Mar 1868
P: Leland, Michigan

(Spouse of no. 1)

24 James Whiton
C: 13 Aug 1651
M:
D:

12 Joseph Whiton
B: 23 Mar 1687
P: Hingham, MA
M: 19 Dec 1713
P: Hingham, MA
D: 1777
P: Ashford, Windham, CT

25 Abigail Rickard
B: 1655
D: 4 May 1740

6 Elijah Whiton
B: 7 Jul 1714
P: Hingham, MA
M: 23 Nov 1758
P:
D: 20 Aug 1784
P: Ashford, Windham, CT

26 Samuel Tower
B:
M:
D:

13 Martha Tower
B: 20 Jul 1693
P: Hingham, MA
D: 19 Sep 1719
P: Rehoboth, MA

27 Silence Damon
B:
D:

3 Amy Whiton
B: 16 Aug 1773
P: Ashford, Windham, CT
D: 23 May 1853
P: Union, Tolland, CT

28 Eleazer Crocker
B: 21 Jul 1650
M: 7 Apr 1682
D:

14 Eleazer Crocker
B: 3 Aug 1693
P: Barnstable, MA
M:
P:
D:
P:

29 Ruth Chipman
B: Dec 1663
D: 8 Apr 1698

7 Hannah Crocker
B: 27 Jun 1729
P: Windham, Windham, CT
D: 1809
P:

30
B:
M:
D:

15 Judith Sanders
B: 17 Jun 1696
P: Haverhill, Essex, MA
D: 26 Aug 1776
P:

31
B:
D:

Prepared by
Isabel Weigold
48 Red Oak Hill
Willington, CT 06279

Telephone

Date prepared
3 Apr 2005

# Pedigree Chart = D

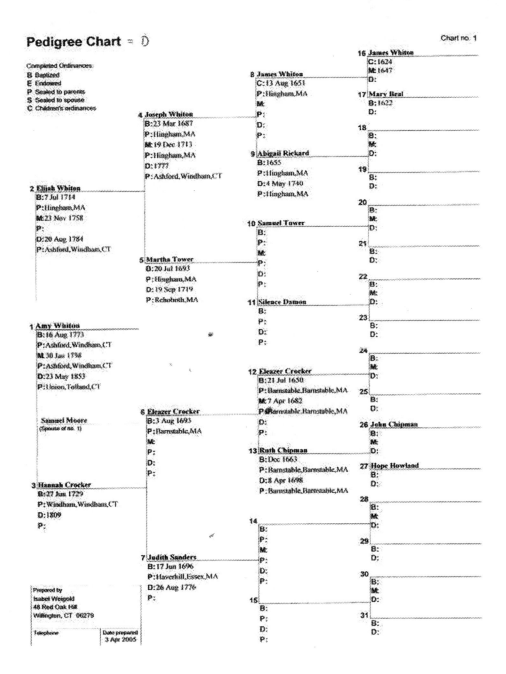

Completed Ordinances:
B Baptized
E Endowed
P Sealed to parents
S Sealed to spouse
C Children's ordinances

16 **James Whiton**
C: 1624
M: 1647
D:

8 **James Whiton**
C: 13 Aug 1651
P: Hingham, MA
M:
P:
D:
P:

17 **Mary Beal**
B: 1622
D:

4 **Joseph Whiton**
B: 23 Mar 1687
P: Hingham, MA
M: 19 Dec 1713
P: Hingham, MA
D: 1777
P: Ashford, Windham, CT

18
B:
M:
D:

9 **Abigail Rickard**
B: 1655
P: Hingham, MA
D: 4 May 1740
P: Hingham, MA

19
B:
D:

2 **Elijah Whiton**
B: 7 Jul 1714
P: Hingham, MA
M: 23 Nov 1758
P:
D: 20 Aug 1784
P: Ashford, Windham, CT

20
B:
M:
D:

10 **Samuel Tower**
B:
P:
M:
P:
D:
P:

21
B:
D:

5 **Martha Tower**
D: 20 Jul 1693
P: Hingham, MA
D: 19 Sep 1719
P: Rehoboth, MA

22
B:
M:
D:

11 **Silence Damon**
B:
P:
D:
P:

23
B:
D:

1 **Amy Whiton**
B: 16 Aug 1773
P: Ashford, Windham, CT
M: 30 Jan 1798
P: Ashford, Windham, CT
D: 23 May 1853
P: Union, Tolland, CT

24
B:
M:
D:

12 **Eleazer Crocker**
B: 21 Jul 1650
P: Barnstable, Barnstable, MA
M: 7 Apr 1682
P: Barnstable, Barnstable, MA
D:
P:

25
B:
D:

6 **Eleazer Crocker**
B: 3 Aug 1693
P: Barnstable, MA
M:
P:
D:
P:

26 **John Chipman**
B:
M:
D:

**Samuel Moore**
(Spouse of no. 1)

13 **Ruth Chipman**
B: Dec 1663
P: Barnstable, Barnstable, MA
D: 8 Apr 1698
P: Barnstable, Barnstable, MA

27 **Hope Howland**
B:
D:

3 **Hannah Crocker**
B: 27 Jun 1729
P: Windham, Windham, CT
D: 1809
P:

28
B:
M:
D:

14
B:
P:
M:
P:
D:
P:

29
B:
D:

7 **Judith Sanders**
B: 17 Jun 1696
P: Haverhill, Essex, MA
D: 26 Aug 1776
P:

30
B:
M:
D:

15
B:
P:
D:
P:

31
B:
D:

Prepared by
Isabel Weigold
48 Red Oak Hill
Willington, CT 06279

Telephone

Date prepared
3 Apr 2005

Hannah Moore, a native of Union, Connecticut, was inspired to become a missionary by the story of the enforced march of the Cherokees, referred to as the "Trail of Tears." She dedicated her life to that cause, serving at the Dwight Mission in what was then the Oklahoma Territory, teaching the Cherokee and Choctaw Indians to read and write. She knew John Ross, the chief of the Cherokees at the time.

Later she went to Kaw Mendi, Africa, where she heard the story of the "return of the Amistad" as told by the men and women who had been captured and imprisoned aboard that ship and later tried in New Haven, Connecticut.

Isabel Weigold found one of Hannah's letters in the Willington Historical Society archives which referred to the "return of the Amistad." After five years of research in which she uncovered over one hundred letters written by Hannah or about her, Isabel has written her story—a story of courage, devotion, and religious zeal under the most trying circumstances.

# ABOUT THE AUTHOR

Born in New Haven, Connecticut, Isabel Beck (Miller) Weigold received most of her early education in the East Haven, Connecticut, schools. When the country became engaged in World War II, she left her secretarial position with the G&O Manufacturing Co. to join the U.S. Navy (WAVES). She served from 1942 to 1946, moving up through the ranks from Seaman 3rd class to Chief Yeoman. Taking advantage of the GI Bill, Mrs. Weigold entered the undergraduate program at the University of Connecticut in 1947. She later went on to get her MA in Educational Psychology and was the school psychologist at Hall Memorial School in Willington, Connecticut, from 1974 until 1987, when she retired.

In 1985, Mrs. Weigold received a Certificate of Commendation from the American Association for State and Local History and the Connecticut League of Historical Organizations in recognition of her research which was the basis for a history of Willington, Connecticut. The book that was born from her research is titled *A Modernization in a New England Town, A History of Willington, Connecticut*, and it was written by Ronald Demers in 1983.

She was appointed town historian by the Board of Selectmen in 1992, a position she still occupies to date. Both she and her husband, Harold, received a Community Service Award in 1995, "In recognition and appreciation for many years of outstanding community service to the Town of Willington." In 2004, she was chosen by the Willington Board of Education to receive the Citizenship Award, in recognition of "her many years of volunteer service to the community activities and organizations of Willington, Connecticut."

Mrs. Weigold is a charter member of the Willington Historical Society, established in 1968, and has been actively involved in researching, writing, and publishing several books concerning Willington's history.

978-0-595-43135-9
0-595-43135-6

Printed in the United States
93681LV00004B/1-198/A